Railway Book

Edited by BRIAN MORRISON & HANDEL KARDAS

LONDON

IAN ALLAN LTD

First published 1991

ISBN 0 7110 2030 2

© Ian Allan Ltd 1991

Published by Ian Allan Ltd, Shepperton, Surrey; and printed by Ian Allan Printing Ltd at their works at Coombelands in Runnymede, England

Front cover:
No 91006 waits patiently at King's Cross for its next turn of duty. *Brian Morrison*

Rear cover, top:
Ex-LMS Class 3F 0-6-0T No 47279 powers its way out of Keighley.

Rear cover, bottom:
A Class 128 diesel parcel unit heads a rake of Class 127 units at St Pancras. *Brian Morrison*

Previous page:
The long history of Stratford Works was scheduled to come to an end in 1991 with closure notices having been served during 1990. On 13 July 1990, the premises are still a hive of industry with Class 31/1 No 31107 and Class 47/4 No 47501 *Craftsman*, among many other locomotives, receiving attention. *Brian Morrison*

Below:
The look of the 1990s at King's Cross on 26 April. Three Class 91s and a solitary Class 43 form various arrivals and departures with, from left to right, Nos 91004 *The Red Arrows*, 91010, 43159 and 91007. *Brian Morrison*

Contents

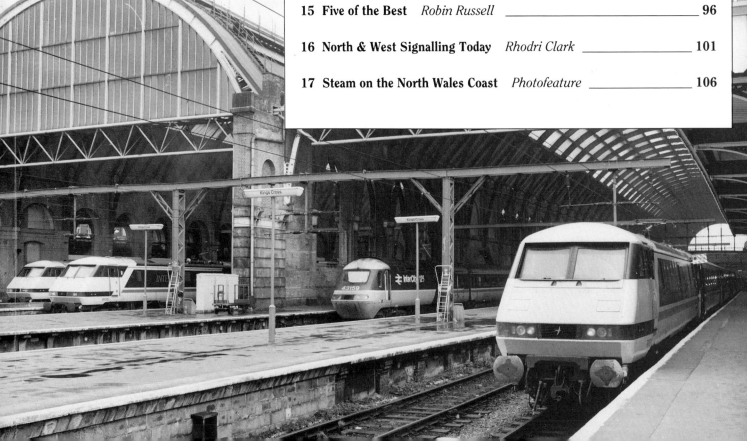

1

A Year in Camera

Brian Morrison

All photographs by the author unless otherwise credited

The year 1989 went out in fine style with a grand tunnel breakthrough for the new Stansted Airport link, commencement of the new Slade Green Depot for the Network SouthEast (NSE) 'Networker' fleet of Class 4EPB replacement EMUs, Railfreight Distribution's Class 86/6s and Class 90s being unveiled, the naming of a Class 56 at Euston complete with attendant coal wagons, a mock-up at London Victoria of the new Class 471 'Networker Express' to replace the 4CEP EMUs, the opening of Guildford's new station and the very successful Windsor Gala Day — and it is rumoured that there was even a whiff of steam at Shepperton on one dark December night!

As the new year dawned, traffic had finally ceased on the old Watlington branch to Chinnor, the Class 60s had begun trials from a number of depots, and the last-ever train departed Holborn Viaduct. A number of Tinsley-allocated Class 37s and 47s in old blue livery were brightened up a little with the addition of unofficial aircraft and bird names, and once familiar nomenclature such as *Wild Swan*, *Sparrow Hawk*, *Bittern* and *Kestrel*

was again on view, albeit quite short-lived in some instances as their owners were repainted into Sector colours.

As weeks went by, it was possible to observe Class 90s on London, Tilbury & Southend metals, see a Class 33 converted to a Driving Van Trailer (DVT) and painted into InterCity Sector colours, witness commencement of the Docklands Light Railway extension to Beckton and the breakthrough of its tunnel to Bank, and celebrate overdue government authorisation of a Liverpool Street-Paddington cross-London link together with a further DLR extension across the River Thames to Lewisham — and not forgetting the switch-on for the 'Solent Link' electric services joining Portsmouth with Eastleigh and Southampton and incorporating a new station at Hedge End. With the elimination

Below:

The 14.35 empty hoppers from Exeter Riverside (7V84) heads for Meldon Quarry on 14 September and passes Gunstone Mills, near Yeoford, powered by Class 33/1 'Bagpipes' Nos 33108 and 33114. Liveries were again well to the fore during 1990, the leading locomotive here being in Departmental grey with the upper half of the bodysides newly coloured yellow to signify that it is allocated to the Civil Engineer's pool.

of Holborn Viaduct and the emergence of St Paul's Thameslink to take its place, the remarkable building works and track realignment to Blackfriars were completed, and at the same time 'Thameslink' services were extended to include Guildford, and the major refurbishments and developments at Charing Cross, Cannon Street, Liverpool Street, Paddington and Waterloo stations either neared completion or began to take shape. In Scotland, the Kilmacolm line which closed in January 1983 was reopened as far as Paisley Canal, and in the Midlands, new stations were opened at Bloxwich North and Tame Bridge; Whiston, Worle, and Woodsmoor stations were new additions to the Merseyrail, Bristol, and Greater Manchester networks, respectively, and four-platformed Meadowhall Interchange, north of Sheffield, and Walsden, on the Manchester-Caldervale line, opened in Yorkshire. Twenty-five years after it was closed by Dr Beeching, Steeton & Silsden station was reopened by West Yorkshire Passenger Transport Executive (PTE) and a limited service was introduced between Preston, Blackburn and Clitheroe by Network NorthWest, with a weekly 'Dalesrail' train extended to Hellifield to join with the Settle & Carlisle route. Three years of trains to Corby, however, came to an end when the

Above:

The scene at a wet Glasgow Central on 18 September 1990, with Railfreight Distribution Class 90 No 90046, engaged on mileage accumulation, preparing to depart with the 11.35 'Sussex Scot' for Brighton. Also to be seen in the platforms are Class 303 EMUs forming Cathcart Circle services and a Class 318 with a train for Gourock.

Right:

As 1989 closed, a full-size mock-up of the Class 471 'Networker Express' EMU, which Network SouthEast hoped to introduce during 1992/93, was unveiled for public viewing and comment at London Victoria station. Intended to replace the 31-year-old Class 411 4CEP units currently used on Kent Coast services to Dover and Ramsgate, the project was put on to the back burner some 10 months later due to funding being unavailable as a result of the costs to be incurred by the forthcoming cross-London line from Paddington to Liverpool Street, announced at the Conservative party conference.

Right:

Class 60 No 60010 *Pumlumon/Plynlimon* hauls Redland Aggregates hoppers on a run past at Coalville during the depot's very successful Open Day on 3 June.

Facing page, bottom:

Named *United Transport Europe* at Cowley, Oxford, on 5 July, Class 47/0 No 47218 is a Railfreight Distribution locomotive allocated to Tinsley depot.

local council withdrew its line subsidy to BR in order to reduce its Poll Tax (sorry, community charge) and left BR economically unable to continue the service. Should proposed new Swindon-Peterborough trains come about, however, it is possible that the station could once again come alive.

Towards the end of the year, the 1,000th train of concrete segments for the Channel Tunnel left the Isle of Grain site, and the tunnel itself was constantly in the news, mostly for all the wrong reasons. It would seem that things have gone too far to turn back now, however, as apart from the tunnel workings from both England and France having met, massive sites are under construction for European trains at Dollands Moor and Holywell Combe, near Folkestone, and at North Pole Junction in West London, where the loop to Old Oak Common has been eliminated in addition to Mitre Bridge and North Pole signalboxes.

Names of Note
Apart from the unofficial Tinsley namings which have been mentioned, and the myriad of nameplates in English, Scottish and Welsh affixed to the new Class 60 fleet, there was considerable activity in the naming game during 1990, with just one Class 60 having an official naming ceremony to commemorate the founder of the Salvation Army, *William Booth*, no fewer than 12 Class 47s losing their plates and another 15 gaining new ones, plus the restoration of *North Star*, missing for nearly two years. Notable losses included *Great Eastern*, *Springburn*, *Stratford*, *Sir Walter Scott*, *Sir Daniel Gooch*, *Saint Andrew*, *London Standard*, and two of the dedicated Shell petroleum Stanlow oil fleet, all as a result of a material reallocation of Sector. *The Gloucestershire Regiment*, *Pegasus*, *Derby Evening Telegraph*, *Sir Rowland Hill*, *University of Oxford*, *Ruskin College Oxford*, and *Royal Engineer's Postal & Courier Services* are now sported by Class 47s in a variety of liveries, together with commercial connections such as *Blue Circle Cement*, *Civil Link*, *Track 29*, *Distillers MG*,

Transmark and *United Transport Europe*. Selhurst Depot unofficially christened some of its Class 415/4 4EPB charges with various girls' names, a Class 09 shunter was officially named *Three Bridges C.E.D.*, and two Class 31s also received names (*Jerome K. Jerome* and *The Enginemen's Fund*), but three lost them, The number of named examples of the class actually increased by one, however, as again due to sector transfers, the lost names were transferred to other locomotive's within the fleet; the exception was *Amlwch Freighter*, now adorning a Class 47. A Class 86/2 originally named *Harold Macmillan* was given the name *Norwich Festival*, and another of the same class which had carried the name *Novelty* since June 1979 was renamed *Harold Macmillan*. On the basis that a novelty cannot last forever, these plates are presumably now for sale, unless they are to adorn one of a number of still unnamed Class 86/4s!

The policy of giving Class 56s business names linking them to Railfreight Sector customers continued, and the policy of removing far more Class 43 powercar names than ever seems likely to be restored, also continued. Among others, new-style InterCity Sector plates were unveiled for *The Royal Regiment of Wales*, *TSW Today*, *Swan Hunter*, *County of Cornwall*, *Granite City* and *City of Discovery* (Aberdeen and Dundee respectively), but many more HST powercars await return of nameplates which were removed, in some cases, well over two years ago. Some locomotives of the Class 90 and 91 fleets are receiving names but, unfortunately, these are also of the new InterCity type which still look tinny, are still reflective and are still difficult to see. *The Red Arrows* and *Terence Cuneo* have rightly been honoured with Class 91s bearing their name, together with *Scottish Enterprise*, the first of the type to cross the border. Class 90s have received such diverse names as the strangely colloquial The *Liverpool Phil*, a formal *The Birmingham Royal Ballet*, the somewhat over-the-top *Glasgow 1990 — Cultural Capital of Europe* and the pleasant *Penny Black*.

Two further Class 442 'Wessex Electrics' have been named *County of Dorset* and *Thomas Hardy*, and two Class 73s which had been named *Poste Haste* and *Quadrant* lost their plates, the former one now adorning a Parcels Sector Class 86/4, with the latter due to be remounted on another locomotive in 1991. Despite their nameplate losses, named Class 73 electro-diesels maintained their numbers, however, with two receiving the plates *University of Kent at Canterbury* and *Battle of Britain 50th Anniversary*. Previous prolific namings of Class 37s slowed considerably with just four receiving plates during the year, *Sir William Arrol* (builder of the Forth Bridge), *British International Freight Association*, *The Lass o' Ballochmyle* (nameplates over 8ft in length!) and *Westerleigh*, the naming of which, for reasons unknown, was steeped in mystery with the railway press being excluded.

Motive Power Movements
A variety of technical problems encountered with the introduction of Class 158 'Express' DMUs and Railfreight Class 60s resulted in some pleasure for the railway enthusiast but dismay for BR, and in some cases, despair for long-suffering customers. Without the expected new locomotives, Railfreight Sector was obliged to retain a number of older types in order to maintain its business, and although some had to be withdrawn during the year, many more than originally anticipated remained in service and had money expended upon them to keep them running. Network SouthEast Sector's main problems arose as the year came to an end, when availability of Class 50s was at its lowest ever ebb, and Class 33s were drafted back on to West of England services together with Departmental 50s, Class 47/4s from Parcels, Intercity and NSE, and even the occasional 'Thumper' DEMU was utilised at least as far as Salisbury. Provincial Sector (which was renamed Regional Railways in December) had all manner of problems trying to maintain passenger services with life-expired diesel units; in some instances it was felt necessary to cancel

Above:
On 17 February, driver training train 6G50, the 09.56 Temple Mills-Ipswich and return, approaches Dagenham Dock with InterCity-liveried Class 90 No 90025 hauling a train of 15 HEA coal hoppers.

Below:
During the early part of 1990, the 09.30 Sunday train from Oxford to Paddington was booked for a pair of Class 50s. On 11 February, the rostered locomotives passing Southall are No 50023 *Howe* and No 50035 *Ark Royal*, both in the revised version of NSE livery incorporating a darker colour blue and without the upward colour sweep at the front. Later in the year, Old Oak Common depot lost the last of its allocated 'Hoovers' to Laira and all 'Network Expresses' on the Oxford route were worked by Class 47s.

some timetabled trains and, in others, resort was made to ancient Class 20s and 31s, together with slightly less-ancient Class 37s, with hauled coaching stock being utilised for Crewe-Derby turns, and for workings between Manchester and Southport, Barrow and Blackpool, Liverpool and Preston and Bristol and Weymouth, all of which had extra passengers, as enthusiasts swelled the numbers of the more usual travellers. The year in detail for BR DMUs appears as a separate feature.

The financial value of railway enthusiasts (or Gricers, as now officially described in the latest edition of *Chambers English Dictionary*) was evident to British Rail when Class 47s on a number of Leeds-Carlisle trains were specially provided with pilots consisting of a pair of Class 20s or a Class 56 or 58 — and the coaches were packed!

During October 1990, ARC's four General Motors Class 59/1s arrived at Newport Docks and soon commenced working from Whatley Quarry following trials. Ranks of Class 08 shunters diminished to some extent along with Class 20s, 31s, 33s and the popular (at least to the enthusiast) Class 50 'Hoovers' which were replaced on Paddington-Oxford trains by displaced ScotRail push-pull Class 47/7s, mostly repainted into NSE livery. Fewer Class 47s were taken out of service than anticipated, as along with five Class 37s, 10 'Duffs' began modification at BRML Doncaster for dedicated Channel Tunnel duties. The biggest surprise of the year, however, was the announcement that the first Class 56s were to be withdrawn in order to provide component exchange with others of the type; the statement, however, was later withdrawn.

The last Class 81 electric locomotives somehow managed to survive into 1991, with their place on empty coaching stock (ecs) workings between Euston and Wembley Depot being supplemented by one of the last two Class 85/0s, the other one being used in a similar capacity at Manchester. The remainder of the Class 85 fleet have been reclassified '85/1' with a 75mph speed limit for Railfreight Sector duties.

The majority of West Coast main line (WCML) InterCity trains were push-pull operated as intended, the electrical controls through the train from Driving Van Trailer (DVT) to locomotive being much more reliable, with far fewer trains being observed with the DVT being dragged behind the locomotive as a result of the Time Division Multiplex (TDM) system failing to work than in 1989. With construction of the Class 90 fleet completed, conversion of Class 86/4 to 86/6 for Railfreight Sector continued apace, with only seven 86/4s scheduled to remain for use

Above:
Ex-Scotrail Mk 2f DBSOs were modified by BREL Derby for use on Liverpool Street-Norwich InterCity services, which went over completely to push-pull operation during 1990. On 1 October, No 9707 heads the 11.30 Liverpool Street-Norwich train passing Witham, propelled at the rear by Class 86/2 No 86220 *The Roundtabler*.

Below:
With newly-laid third rail for the Solent electrification scheme evident at St Denys on 14 February, InterCity long-range fuel tank (ILRA) Class 47/4 No 47840 (ex-47613 *North Star*) hammers through the rain-swept station with the 12.40 service from Poole to Liverpool Lime Street.

as Parcels Sector locomotives. On the East Coast, the Class 91s and their Mk 4 stock continued to impress customers to Leeds and York and the East Coast electrification through to Edinburgh remained within schedule. The Liverpool Street-Norwich/Harwich services went over completely to push-pull operation utilising BREL Derby-modified Mk 2f Driving Brake Standard Open (DBSO) vehicles cascaded from ScotRail Edinburgh-Glasgow expresses following belated introduction of the Class 158s.

With 15 Class 310 EMUs allocated to East Ham Depot, long-suffering London Tilbury & Southend line commuters were treated to haulage by this stock in lieu of the unrefurbished Class 302s which were withdrawn together with the last of the Shenfield Class 307s, although seven of these units live on under the guise of West Yorkshire Passenger Transport Executive (PTE), having been painted into their colours and sent to Leeds Neville Hill, where it was considered that they would go down better with commuters than an overcrowded Pacer!

Friday evening, September 21, was a notable date for London, when the very last train left the capital under semaphore signals, 'Chiltern Line' services from Marylebone now operating under new electric multiple aspect colour lights. As a result of the major resignalling work involved, trains were diverted to Paddington for two weeks.

Class 321s continued to perform well on both 'Northampton Line' and 'Great Eastern' services, which was just as well as their displacement of the popular locomotive-hauled morning and evening 'Cobbler' services to and from Northampton was not initially a popular move. They did, however, encounter problems with single manning in relation to the driver's view of the platform mirrors, as did their similar cousins, the Strathclyde Class 320s and the Stansted Class 322s, both of which were introduced during the year. A contract worth over £500 million for the

purchase of 30 'Three Capitals' Class 373 trains for international services through the Channel Tunnel between London and Paris and London and Brussels was won by a British, Belgium and French consortium led by GEC Alsthom, with the contract for Class 92 dual-voltage locomotive for international freight haulage and overnight passenger trains being awarded to Brush Electrical Machines in partnership with ABB Transportation Systems. The order for the Class 323 EMU for Birmingham cross-city services was won by Hunslet Transportation Projects, who also commenced work on converting the fleet of 35 Class 155/0 'Super Sprinters' into 70 single-car Class 153 'Super Bubblecars'

for use on local and branch line services in non-electrified areas.

On Southern metals, a number of Class 415/1 4EPB slam-door units have been declared life-expired, but many of the sets remaining in service have been fitted with headlamps as a token modernisation until new Class 465 'Networkers' are fully introduced; some 2EPBs also received the fitment together with 4CEP, 4CIG and 4VEP units. Meanwhile the two-car Class 456 version of the 455 fleet arrived, as did newly made-up Class 431 six-car REPs for use in connection with the 'Solent Link' services, and the first of the additional Class 319/1 'Thameslink' EMUs. The 16 dedicated Class 421/5 'Portsmouth Greyhound' 4CIGs were given

their own block of new numbers and a black crescent at the top of the cab front to distinguish them from other 4CIGs which do not have their improved Mk 6 bogies and top speed capability of over 90mph. More Class 411/5 4CEP 'Kent Coasters' then anticipated managed to retain their attractive 'jaffa cake' livery for another year, although a large number did succumb to NSE red, white, blue and grey. Refurbishment of the entire 4VEP fleet neared completion and the only remaining third-rail stock in the old blue and grey colours appeared to be the unrefurbished Class 415/416 slam-door 4EPB/2EPBs, a few Class 414 4CAPs and the one Class 414/2 2HAP. Initial problems with the Class 442 'Wessex Electrics' were resolved although they all lost the jumper-cable covers, to the detriment of their otherwise good looks.

Both Chester and Fratton closed as maintenance depots during the year and notices of closure were served at Stratford, where Level Five maintenance at the major depot is scheduled to finish in March 1991. Stratford was closed once before in 1963, but was reopened again four months later to survive into the 1990s. On this occasion, the demise

seemed at first to be a permanent one, but as the year came to an end it appeared that, in fact, the depot would receive yet another reprieve and remain open after all; perhaps the Stratford cockney sparrow emblem should be changed for one depicting Houdini!

Days of Note
Some factions and individuals within British Rail are of the opinion that the railway enthusiast is an intrusion into their working day and that the railway would be a better place without them. A railway employee found to be an enthusiast can be looked down upon by some in management, and it is not unknown for expected promotion not to materialise and for the individual to be transferred to another position not commensurate with his knowledge and ability. When it come to open days and special events, however, it is usually the railwaymen who are also enthusiasts who take on the workload and arrange everything for railway charities such as Woking Homes and Enginemen's Fund to benefit. During the year, very successful Open Days were again held at Bescot, Cambridge, Coalville, Gloucester and Tinsley, with 'new boys' Barry, Three Bridges and Streatham Hill making their Open Day debut. London Transport also had special events to commemorate the centenary of the world's first deep level tube, with Open Days held at Upminster, Ruislip and Morden Depots, at the first named involving the unlikely sight of steam on the District Line, and the latter including two special trains run by Ian Allan Ltd which was also involved in the very first Network NorthWest Day. MidLine Day was another conspicuous success and the organisation behind NSE's fourth Birthday and its International Flower Show specials, the reopening of the Ness Viaduct and countless other BR Public Affairs functions which took place during the year under review should not be forgotten. The biggest of them all is most unlikely ever to be forgotten, as it has been extensively photo-graphed and chronicled throughout both national and railway press and, in addition, the spectacular bridge illuminations are to last for 10 years. It is hoped that everyone involved in the superb Forth Bridge Centenary celebrations have been given the credit they deserve.

Credits and Debits
An operating loss for BR in 1989 was reported in 1990 and was the first for several years. Reasons propounded included lost revenue from the BR drivers' one-day strikes and a downturn in the country's economy resulting in fewer people travelling while money remained tight. An encouraging view of the future was taken in BR's Annual Report, but the effect of poll tax and inflation was more likely to make things worse in 1990, particularly with reduced property income struggling to keep the overall figures in the black. The effect on the environment contributed by ever more congested roads must be good news for the future of railways generally, but this country still lags well behind the majority of Europe in not permitting BR to compete fairly with both road and air travel; and a prerequisite to show a minium 8% return on all investment does not assist the situation when that investment is from BR's own coffers and not from the taxpayer's pockets.

Sir Bob Reid Mk 1 retired as BR Chairman in 1990 and his place was taken by Sir Bob Reid Mk 2. Mk 1 Sir Bob may be remembered as one of the finest chairmen which BR have ever had. Should Mk 2 Sir Bob do as much for the railway, BR's long term will be secure — despite problems with a seemingly reluctant government who, regardless of a number of shuffles within the Ministry of Transport, are overdue a change of attitude to the railway. Possibly the most striking indication of a change of attitude comes from the USA where in 1978 the state of California instigated what was to become something of a global revolt against taxes when it voted for the now-famous Proposition 13. Now Californians have been campaigning to *raise* their taxes, putting forward a new Proposition 111 which would increase tax on petrol and use the proceeds, primarily to build new railways. A hoarding erected by campaigners above the lines of jammed cars proclaimed: **Had enough traffic? Vote yes on 111.** Amazingly 52% of the voters did say Yes. Where America leads, the United Kingdom follows?

Network Commentary

Facelifting of Phase two Class 421/2 4CIG stock continues slowly, with newly classified 421/4 EMUs fitted with new upholstery, fluorescent lighting and a public address system. One such unit, No 1811, forms the rear of a London Victoria-bound semi-fast service at Brighton, with the destination indicator showing stops at Burgess Hill, Wivelsfield, Haywards Heath, Balcombe, Three Bridges, Gatwick Airport, East Croydon and Clapham Junction.

Southampton Eastern Docks was brought back into occasional use for boat train services during 1990. Seen on the branch between the Docks and Northam Junction on 28 July, Class 73/0 No 73005 *Mid-Hants Watercress Line* hauls the empty coaching stock from the 09.13 train from Kensington Olympia, which is being taken to Eastleigh for servicing.

Left:
Newly painted into NSE livery, Classes 307 and 308/1 EMUs Nos 307111 and 308159 are posed for the camera in Ilford Works Yard on 20 February. Displaced by Class 321s, the 34-year-reign of the Class 307s on Liverpool Street-Southend Victoria services ended on 30 June, after which six of the units went to Neville Hill, Leeds, for West Yorkshire PTE, and the remainder were put into store.

Below:
The 60 Class 319/0 units for 'Thameslink' services are being augmented by 25 similar Class 319/1s, delivery of which commenced in October. Apart from the colour surrounding the yellow front end being white instead of dark gray, other detail differences include the front skirt deflector and the driver's doors which are now of the plug type. The illustration on page 46 provides a comparison with this view of No 319032 leaving St Pancras on a St Albans service on 4 August.

*now you
see them,*

Above:

Following a naming ceremony at Scunthorpe on 19 March, Class 56 No 56102 sports new *Scunthorpe Steel Centenary* plates, and prepares to move away with a haul of HAA Coal Sector hoppers, which are in as equally pristine condition as the locomotive.

Right:

Shortly prior to being repainted into NSE colours, ex-Scotrail Class 47/7 No 47707 *Holyrood* is seen at its new Old Oak Common home on 27 May, alongside Class 47/4 No 47569 which was later given Parcels Sector red/grey livery and named *The Gloucestershire Regiment.*

Left:

At a special ceremony at the Royal Engineer's Resources Depot at Long Marston on 20 March, one of the new nameplates decorating the flanks of Class 47/4 No 47568 is revealed by Mr Bill Cockburn, Managing Director of Royal Mail Letters.

Below left:

The nameplate and Depot crest of *Crewe Diesel Depot* unveiled on Class 47/4 No 47489 during the Coalville Open Day on 3 June.

Below:

One of Tinsley Depot's unofficial names.

LATES
now you don't.

Above right:

Named *The Liverpool Phil* at Lime Street station on 21 March to commemorate 150 years of the Liverpool Philharmonic Orchestra, Class 90 No 90014 worked back to Euston with a special train conveying the orchestra, who gave a concert in London that evening. Arriving at its destination, the locomotive is joined at the adjacent platform by Class 81 No 81017 which is hauling empty coaching stock (ecs) for a later departure; a contrast in the oldest and latest motive power on the West Coast main line (WCML) at this time.

Right:

Given the name *Cricklewood* to commemorate that depot upon its closure, Class 31/1 No 31307 lost the plates during the year, which later reappeared on another member of the class, No 31102, but retained its white body stripe. Passing Goodmayes on 8 February hauling three 'Carless' tanks to Harwich Parkestone Quay, the scars left when the nameplates were removed can be seen quite clearly.

Left:

Having pulled the cord to reveal the nameplates which now adorn Class 73/1 No 73112, the University of Kent's Pro-Chancellor, Dr David Say, accepts a replica plate from NSE's South East District Manager, Geoff Harrison-Mee, at Canterbury West station on 3 April.

Below:

Coal Sector Class 37/5 No 37693 provides the unusual sight of loaded HAA merry-go-round hoppers under the Edinburgh Waverley station roof on 23 March. As part of the Forth Bridge centenary celebrations, the locomotive was named *Sir William Arrol*, the structure's builder.

Railfreight Trainload

Above:
On a sunny 8 June, Toton's Yorkshire Coal Sector FEDN Class 56 No 56069 rasps through Doncaster station hauling empty merry-go-round HAA hoppers.

Right:
Carrying Construction Sector decals, FASB Class 33/0 No 33051 *Shakespeare Cliff* stands in Hither Green depot yard on 19 February at the head of a line-up of other class members, most of which are mainly engaged upon duties in connection with Channel Tunnel construction.

Below right:
Stopped on the centre road at Shrewsbury on 29 June for a crew change, Mirrlees-engined FMHK Class 37/9 No 37904 heads the Railfreight Steel 07.10 Llanwern-Dee Marsh coil train. The locomotive has the correct decal indicating Steel Sector on the cabside, but the main bodyside ones are missing.

Facing page, top:
Powering an extremely long test train from Mountsorrel to Cricklewood through Silkstream Junction on 17 May, Class 60 No 60001 *Steadfast* carries Construction Sector decals, while No 60002 *Capability Brown* displays those of Petroleum Sector. *Brian Beer*

Facing page, bottom:
Allocated to the FCTY Pool for Thornaby-allocated Railfreight Chemicals locomotives, Class 47/3 No 47305 emerges from Hallam Oil Terminal at Bromsgrove on 17 September with a haul of tanks for Port Clarence (6E55), and successfully diverts the attention of guests on Bromsgrove station who are attending the celebrations going on that morning in connection with the 150th anniversary of the Lickey incline, as shown overleaf.

New for the 1990s

Above:

A new platform, station footbridge, and much improved services were announced for Bromsgrove on 17 September at the same time as 'Lickey 150' was celebrated by taking invited guests up and down the famous hill in Class 121 'Midline' liveried 'bubble car' No 55033.

Right:

A light haul of three PCA Presflo wagons for nearby Bescot is taken through newly-opened Tame Bridge station on 4 June, hauled by Class 37/0 No 37045. This locomotive was one regeared with CP7 bogies and redesignated 37/3, with number 37355, but later returned to original condition with its first TOPS number reinstated.

Below right:

The old Glasgow & South Western Railway route from Glasgow Buchanan Street to Greenock Princes Pier was truncated at Kilmacolm in February 1959, becoming a branch line from Shields, eventually served from Glasgow Central. The branch closed completely for passenger traffic in January 1983, but it was realised that too much had been removed and it was reopened again as far as a re-sited Paisley Canal station in July. This gave Strathclyde's railways a new station at Dumbreck and reopened others at Corkerhill, Mosspark, Crookston and later, Hawkhead. On 18 September, a cyclist is grateful that he does not have to pedal any further through the rain as he dismounts at the Canal terminus to put his machine into the guard's compartment of Class 156 'Super Sprinter' No 156512, forming the 11.06 service to Glasgow Central.

Above:
The first of the second batch of 26 'Thameslink' EMUs was delivered in October and quickly put to work. Following complaints from the more affluent Brighton commuters, first-class accommodation is now provided, and the appearance in Kent, therefore, of a Class 319/1 will not be common. On 15 November, unit No 319161 passes Bickley Junction forming the 10.38 Sevenoaks-Luton train.

Right:
Headlights began to appear on a variety of motive power during the year, to include unlikely Southern Region suburban EMU slam-door stock. With new light aglow, Class 415/4 4EPB No 5464 heads away from Polhill tunnel, near Dunton Green, on 6 November with an ecs working for Chart Leacon Works.

Below right:
Constructed similarly to the successful Class 321 fleet, Class 320 EMUs for Strathclyde services entered traffic in the summer with the intention of displacing non-refurbished Pressed Steel Co Class 303 stock and the remaining Cravens Class 311s. On 19 September, units Nos 320315/318 pass Yoker station on driver training.

Above:
The four new Class 59/1 locomotives ordered from General Motors, USA, by Associated Roadstone Co (Southern) arrived at Newport Docks on 20 October and are seen here lined up on the quayside following off-loading. Reading from the left, they are Nos 59101, 59104, 59103 and 59102.   *Colin J. Marsden*

Left:
Ex-Class 33/1 No 33115 was converted to a Driving Van Trailer (DVT) at RFS Projects, Doncaster, for a new role as bogie testing vehicle for Channel Tunnel trains. Renumbered 83301, the machine stands inside Stewarts Lane Depot on 1 March, dressed up in InterCity livery and awaiting its first run attached to a 4TC unit with power provided by a Class 73 electro-diesel.

Below left:
The first Southern Region unit to be fitted with a headlight in addition to marker/tail lights, Class 421/5 4CIG 'Greyhound' No 1315 is displayed outside BRML Eastleigh on 9 May. Dedicated for express Waterloo-Portsmouth Harbour services, the fleet of 16 units have all been renumbered into a 13XX series.

Above right:
Seen in the 'small hours' at Perth on 19 September, Class 158 units Nos 158717/718 are working a mileage accumulation test run while, to the rear, No 158703 is in use for staff training.

Right:
As many London, Tilbury & Southend passenger services as possible went over to Class 310 motive power during 1990, with the initial 15 units allocated to East Ham Depot being supplemented by others of the class as they were released from Great Eastern rostas by incoming Class 317/2s from the Great Northern Lines. On 1 October, units Nos 310093/097 approach Grays forming the 17.26 service from Fenchurch Street to Tilbury Riverside.

Left:
One of Derby Research Centre's Class 47/4s, No 47972, comes down the hill from Sharnbrook summit on 30 March hauling Mk 4 DVT No 82209 and new Mk 4 stock on delivery from BREL Derby to Bounds Green Depot for East Coast main line (ECML) InterCity services.

Below:
Stage one of the scheme to construct Waterloo's International terminus for Channel Tunnel trains was to provide for additional platforms to accommodate the Windsor Lines which were being replaced by the new building. The old taxi road was the first part of the station to be rebuilt, and it was brought into use as platforms 12 and 13, with other platforms being suitably renumbered. On 22 August, 'Hoover' No 50028 *Tiger* rests at the buffer-stops of platform 13 having brought in the 10.20 train from Exeter St Davids.

Diversions

Above:
Due to engineer's possession in the Wimbledon area on 28 April, Waterloo-bound services were diverted through Byfleet and Addlestone Junctions, via Chertsey and Staines, and regained their normal route again at Clapham Junction, having travelled through some unlikely locations such as this one at Virginia Water, where the 10.20 Exeter St Davids-Waterloo 'Network Express; is powered by the 'green machine', Class 50 No 50007 *Sir Edward Elgar*.

Left:
Major line-speed upgrading on the West Coast main line at Weedon involved engineer's possession for two weekends in June, with all main line services between Euston and Rugby diverted through Northampton. On 17 June, the 10.30 Euston-Manchester Piccadilly train approaches Nothampton station hauled by Class 90 No 90021.

Left:
BR's order for 23 Class AL1 electric locomotives for the newly-electrified WCML to Liverpool and Manchester was placed with AEI who sub-contracted the mechanical construction to the Birmingham Railway Carriage & Wagon Co (BRCW) who completed the first locomotive for hand-over in November 1959. Given the classification 81 at the TOPS renumbering scheme, the last two locomotives of the type were scheduled for final withdrawal from service during 1990, working their last days on London ecs workings. As things transpired, however, Nos 81012 and 81017 were required to soldier on to see the dawn of yet another year. Just prior to withdrawal on 13 May, one of the type that was finally put out to grass, 30 years old No 81004, still decorated with the Scottish salmon emblem from its days at Glasgow Shields Road, comes to a halt at the Euston buffer-stops with ecs from Wembley Depot.

Below left:
Holborn Viaduct station opened on 2 March 1874 and closed for ever on 26 January 1990, being replaced by St Paul's Thameslink (see page 10). The very last train to leave the station was a special, completete with headboard, which departed at 19.40 on the final day and travelled to Charing Cross via Victoria, Beckenham Junction and Cannon Street, formed of Class 411/5 4CEPs Nos 1605 and 1513, seen here preparing to depart.

Top:
Following withdrawal, Class 20 No 20188 was obtained by BR's Eastern Counties Training School at Ilford for training purposes. It was hoped that it would be possible for the locomotive to be restored to original condition and possibly used for special traffic in the same way as the celebrity Class 25 *Tamworth Castle*.

Above:
With video cameras fitted to the corners, Class 158 Express DMU No 158714 travelled the British countryside at length during the summer and autumn months conducting gauging tests. On 11 September, it travelled to the West Country and is seen running alongside the sea wall at the classic location of Dawlish. *David Franklin*

Above left:
The Traction and Rolling Stock Maintenance Depot at Fratton closed following completion of the Solent electrification scheme, with the motive power allocated there transferred to Eastleigh and Wimbledon Depots. In pouring rain on 14 February, Class 412/3 4BEP No 2304 is inside the building with Class 423/1 4VEP No 3429 getting wet on the outside.

Left:
Initial problems with the Class 442 fleet, particularly with the plug doors, resulted in the unflattering nickname of 'Plastic Pigs' being bestowed upon them by some maintenance staff at Bournemouth, and eventually by some passengers. Their troubles over, the 'Wessex Electrics' are rightly the pride of NSE Sector, although some young enthusiasts have now dubbed them 'Porkers'. Whether this embellishment to unit No 2402 *County of Hampshire*, seen at Waterloo on 11 July, is intended to be a plastic pig or a porker is not known, but for sure, it will not be popular with management!

Top left:
With engineering work taking place south of Watford on 18 March, all morning workings in and out of Euston were diesel hauled. Passing a London Underground Bakerloo Line train travelling towards London, the 08.10 Euston-Wolverhampton InterCity service is powered by Class 47/4 No 47584 *County of Suffolk* dragging Class 87/0 No 87002 *Royal Sovereign*. The diesel came off the train at Bletchley.

Centre left:
More diesel dragging of WCML trains occurred on the morning of 17 June when the overhead electric lines were switched out to enable further engineering work to take place in connection with track remodelling at Watford. Class 47/4s were used for all InterCity trains, except the 08.10 Euston-Liverpool Lime Street, which utilised the services of a pair of Stratford's Construction-liveried Class 31/1s Nos 31271 and 31294. Hauling Class 86/2 train locomotive No 86241 *Glenfiddich*, the unusual combination passes Queen's Park.

Bottom left:
Near Cheddington on 28 April, what is believed to be the 11.50 Glasgow Central-Euston InterCity service is unusually powered by Class 85/0 No 85008 hauling Mk 3 DVT No 82103. By the end of the year, only two Class 85/0s remained in traffic, both restricted to 45mph for ecs duties.

Right:
Late delivery of the Class 158s resulted in unexpected services going over to locomotive haulage, including some Cardiff/Bristol-Weymouth turns. On 18 July, the 14.50 Westbury-Weymouth train approaches Maiden Newton powered by Departmental Sector grey-liveried DCWA Pool Class 37/0 No 37142, hauling NSE-liveried stock.

Below:
Locomotive-hauled stock also appeared for a time on some Matlock branch trains. Also with NSE-liveried stock, the 15.40 train from Derby to Matlock on 24 August, departs behind Class 20 No 20139, with No 20160 on the rear of the train as there are no run-round facilities at the other end of the line. Alongside is the late-running 14.23 Sheffield-St Pancras HST.

Specials

Right:
The Southern Electric Group's 'Thanet Explorer' railtour crosses the Kingsferry Bridge on to the Isle of Sheppey on 25 August headed by Railfreight Construction Class 33/0 No 33033, with No 33063 propelling at the rear. The tour commenced from Clapham Junction and travelled via Sheerness, Eastbourne and Tonbridge before returning to its starting point.

Below:
Fully two years after the 'final' Class 50-hauled railtour, No 50020 Revenge operated the 'Taw and Tor Tourer' on 5 May, seen here passing the old station platforms at Okehampton, heading for Meldon Quarry. *Ken Brunt*

Left:
Negotiating Dudding Hill Junction, Cricklewood, on 17 June, Class 47/4 No 47508 SS *Great Britain* hauls a Sunday morning 'Chartex' special (1Z37) from Burton-on-Trent to Portsmouth Harbour.

Left:
The Class 33 Preservation Society's 'Anniversary Aggregate' railtour proceeds carefully down the freight only branch to the Brett Marine aggregate terminal at Cliffe on 6 January, hauled by Class 33/0 No 33051 *Shakespeare Cliff* and propelled by No 33050 *Isle of Grain*. The special train started from Salisbury before dawn, and the itinerary included visiting another freight line to Angerstein Wharf, as well as travelling around the southeast London suburban system and visiting Tonbridge and Hastings.

Below:
Shortage of Class 86/2 motive power on 7 December brought about a special working for Class 90 No 90033 when it was rostered for the 19.25 boat train from Liverpool Street to Harwich Parkestone Quay. In push-pull mode, the 'Mainline'-liveried locomotive, allocated to Crewe for Railfreight Distribution duties, awaits departure time prior to propelling the train away from the London terminus.

Left:

Problems with Class 37/5 No 37671 *Tre Pol and Pen* required that it be taken to Laira Depot, Plymouth, for attention. To save a special journey, the recalcitrant locomotive was attached between Class 37/4 No 37412 (named *Loch Lomond* when allocated to ScotRail) and empty CDA china clay hoppers returning to Marsh Mills. The entourage leaves Lostwithiel up loop on 10 September.

Below left:

Having visited Torquay in connection with the Agatha Christie centenary celebrations, and having 'Miss Marple' and 'Hercule Poirot' aboard in the guise of Joan Hickson and David Suchet, the VSOE returns to Waterloo on 15 September hauled by ILRA Class 47/4 No 47834 *Fire Fly*, seen here passing attractive Cockwood Harbour, near Dawlish.

Top:

Powered by Class 47/4 No 47436, the 'Northolt Salopian' railtour passes Kingswinford Junction on 9 June, travelling on the freight only line between Walsall and Stourbridge, via Dudley Port. *Ken Brunt*

Above:

An unusual sight at Ashford, Kent, on 3 April, as Class 455/8 EMU No 5815 of Selhust Depot passes through the station bound for attention at Chart Leacon Works. The destination blinds show 'Smitham-Wimbledon'!

Left:

One of the most unusual sights of the year was the appearance on NSE South Western Metals on 30 August of a pair of Class 20s hauling the structure gauging train from Derby to Wimbledon Depot. Passing Surbiton after restarting from a signal stop, No 20058 and 20087 approach their destination.

31

2

British Rail DMUs -
The Never-ending Saga

Andred

Photographs by Brian Morrison unless otherwise credited

Listening with care to the words of wisdom from BR's Provincial Sector (now Regional Railways) management this review should start full of praise for the Class 158 'Express' diesel multiple units (DMU). As any followers of the British Rail scene will be aware, introduction of these was long delayed. Instead of May 1989 the full service introduction on the ScotRail Glasgow-Aberdeen route was not possible until October 1990. A few services on the Edinburgh-Glasgow via Falkirk route were operated by these trains from mid-September and completely by mid-October followed by the Edinburgh/Glasgow-Inverness and Edinburgh-Aberdeen services from 5 November. Introduction on other routes for these trains was correspondingly delayed with the North Trans-Pennine, Newcastle-Liverpool, due for January 1991 and the first stage of Western Express, the Cardiff-Portsmouth route, due in March. ScotRail's extensive area of operation was covered by 33 units for 29 diagrams but it must be remembered that further modifications had still to be carried out probably including the engine mountings to reduce saloon noise.

The DMU accolades for 1990 thus go to the Metro-Cammell built Class 156 Super

Sprinters which, during the summer timetable, proved excellent deputies on the ScotRail services. The Class 156 units have been trouble free compared with most new designs of stock introduced on BR in recent years. They were 'borrowed' as they came off the Washwood Heath production lines as their sisters, the Leyland Bus built Class 155s, were withdrawn from Western Express and West Yorkshire PTE duties owing to door faults. As the 155s returned from modifications, the Class 156s were able to return to their planned duties. However, the non-availability of the 158s created problems, as InterCity required their promised Mk 3 coaching stock from the Edinburgh-Glasgow services and Network SouthEast wanted the Class 47/7 locomotives — in both cases other life-expired rolling stock needed to be condemned and replaced by cascading

Below:
Arriving back at Swindon following a test run to Gloucester on 29 March, Class 158 Express units Nos 158704/701 were 'stopped' following their failure to successfully activate some track circuits en route. Bearing a 'Not to be moved' dolly, the two DMUs are passed by the 11.36 Swansea-Paddington HST, led by Class 43 powercar No 43142, which once carried the nameplates *St Mary's Hospital Paddington.*

stock from other services. Although only capable of 75mph the Class 156s generally maintained schedules for 90mph DMUs or 100mph locomotive-hauled trains with the assistance of the Civil Engineer restricting track maintenance to night periods and keeping speed restrictions to a minimum. The 158s were used for mileage accumulation trials, but firstly they could not be relied on to operate track circuits, and then the rolling stock engineers decided that the riding quality at high speeds was not good enough and that the yaws and dampers required modification. The first problem had been previously experienced with Pacer units and was overcome by fitting a Track Circuit Actuator (TCA), but the other problem was a 'drawing board' one. Until modified with the TCA, all movements of the 158s had to be with another Sprinter class unit (150-156) attached and only the Class 154 was suitable for high sped (90mph) test running. During July, Class 158 No 158714 was fitted with cameras for checking clearances at stations and other strategic points on the planned routes of operation on Anglia, Eastern, Midland and Southern Regions. In September it made two appearances at London Waterloo. This was followed in October by two sets being used to convey MPs on a demonstration trip from Waterloo to Exeter culminating in an announcement from the Secretary

Above:

The 12.25 North West-East Anglia service from Liverpool Lime Street to Cambridge makes the prescribed stop at Ely on 17 January, formed of Metro-Cammell Class 156 Super Sprinter No 156414. Compared with most new stock designs introduced on BR in recent years, these units have been relatively trouble free.

Left:

Phase one of a programme of station improvements in Lancashire was completed in December 1989 with the opening of refurbished Huncoat station, seen here with a red and cream-liveried West Yorkshire PTE Class 155/1 No 155342 passing through as the 09.51 service from York to Blackpool North. This is one of only seven Class 155/1 DMUs which are scheduled to remain in original form, the other 35 two-car Class 155/0 units being converted to Class 153 single-car trains by fitting an additional cab.

Below left:

The lone Class 154 Sprinter No 154002 makes the Derby stop as the 12.43 Lincoln-Birmingham New Street service. During the period that the Class 158s had problems activating track circuits, this unit was the only one capable of test running with them at speeds of up to 90mph.

of State for Transport that NSE had been given outline approval to purchase 72 vehicles, classified 159, for this route. In fact 66 of the vehicles are the tail-end of the original Provincial Sector's orders for Class 158s but with interior changes including First Class and the higher powered, 400hp, Cummins engines. They are expected to be formed into three-car sets and be introduced to the route in May 1992. New Class 158 units were provided in October for crew and artisan training at Heaton (Newcastle), York, Edge Hill (Liverpool), Cardiff and Fratton (Portsmouth) and No 158738 took over the clearance tests. BR and the privatised BREL have placed a lot of faith in these trains with a total of 453 vehicles replacing vast quantities of locomotive-hauled and first generation DMU stock. Daily availability figures for

1991 and beyond will have to be 90% plus, with diagrammed mileages of 750-1,000 commonplace. Anything less will be unacceptable.

A new duty for Class 156 units was introduced in October when four three-car units were formed to replace locomotive-hauled trains on the Settle and Carlisle route. First reports suggested they were being used on Trans-Pennine duties, leaving two-car units to the S&C. Shortage of stock precluded their use in three-car sets on the West Highland line this summer with the considerable tourist trade frequently having to turn to BR hired buses due to heavy overcrowding. After some 15 months without a through service between Inverness and the Far North, due to the 1989 floods, services resumed in May and the temporary maintenance depot at Muir of Ord which had coped remarkably well with five Class 156 units, four Class 37/4 locomotives, the Hebridean and InterCity VIP coaching sets and some spare coaches for 15 months, closed and staff returned to Inverness. In October Class 156 units were reintroduced to Aberdeen-Inverness duties with one through working each way to Thurso. Time is allowed at Inverness station to refill the toilet water tank.

The BR Board approved conversion of the 35 two-car Class 155/0 units to 70 Class 153 single car trains by fitting an additional cab and interior changes so that both vehicles have toilets and wheelchair spaces. The contract was awarded in July to Hunslet-Barclay, Kilmarnock, with the first unit, which had collision damage, moving north at the beginning of August. This unit was not due to be returned during 1990. The Class 155/0 units are scheduled for long-term replacement by the Class 158s during 1991, commencing in March. The Class 153s will be used on branch lines in Anglia, the North East, West of England, West Midlands and West Wales.

The most coulourful scene on passenger carrying rolling stock has been in the North West of England. Normally the standard Provincial Sector blue livery, in its varying forms, can be seen on Classes 142, 150/1, 150/2 and 156 with some 'Roses' services being formed of West Yorkshire PTE crimson liveried Classes 144 and 155/1. The former Class 142 Cornish 'Skippers' in chocolate and cream have not been repainted apart from the addition of the Network NorthWest logo. InterCity and the old blue and grey liveries also abound. However, the strangest sights worked from Liverpool Edge Hill Downhill coaching stock depot and Chester DMU depot. Edge Hill is officially operated by InterCity, but over 100 coaches, substantially surplus red, white and blue-liveried stock from Network SouthEast, in some cases with the branding removed, were allocated here by Provincial Sector to deputise for the shortage of DMUs on local services such as Manchester-Southport, Barrow, Blackpool and the Liverpool-Cardiff route. At Chester some Class 101 DMUs painted in Strathclyde PTE orange livery, displaced in Scotland, arrived in May and had the PTE insignia painted out and were paired to work with blue and grey coaches. Some intermediate trailers were included in the stock sent south

but did not operate in service. These sights were partly due to the Class 158 situation and also the poor availability of the Class 142 'Pacer' railbuses. When Chester closed as a maintenance depot at the end of September, its fleet of Classes 101 and 108 was distributed to Tyseley and Longsight. By mid-October, ScotRail was able to release its last five Class 101 sets in passenger use, retaining just two pairs for rail cleaning duties. BR continued its policy of replacing the troublesome SCG gearboxes by the German-produced Voith transmission on Classes 142, 143 and 144 Pacers but a variety of problems continued to leave approximately 25% out of traffic, instead of the norm of around 10% expected for maintenance and repaints on a new fleet; BR called in independent consulting engineers to work out the best methods of remedying the faults. The highly reliable Class 150/2 Sprinters had problems of rotting floors caused by coolant leaks, but progress on repairs was very slow — at least four different workshops (BREL Derby, York, BR Birkenhead and BRML Doncaster) have been used. No reference to colour and Sprinters for 1990 could go without commenting on the new Centro (West Midlands PTE) livery launched in October on Class 150/1 No 150116, followed in November by Class 150/2 No 150202. Large expanses of apple green and white with a Provincial dark blue band and large yellow-backed Centro emblem, not forgetting the orange safety line, provided the most startlingly colourful livery seen in many years. A total of 82 vehicles will be so painted at BRML Eastleigh, but the change is far more than cosmetic. The interior has been re-panneled and reseated with large but discreetly positioned litter bins, also substantial handles by the doorways giving a vital aid for elderly and disabled passengers. The two-car Class 150/2 sets, which unlike the first series have through gangway connections, will be divided to form some three-car Class 150/1 units. The formation will be semi-permanent to allow reversion if required at a later date.

One DMU vehicle had to be withdrawn following a serious accident whilst in public service at Reading, and at least two such accidents with Class 156s necessitated an extended period out of service at BRML Doncaster for rebuilding. Less serious accidents, and a fire at Old Oak Common, London, which destroyed two vehicles, caused a few other vehicles to be withdrawn. Provincial Sector finally cleared its fleet of all asbestos insulated DMUs for passenger service, but insufficient replacements in good enough condition were available for Network South-East to dispose of its few, allocated to three of its four DMU depots. More were allocated to Cambridge as the Sector ceased through working between Liverpool Street and King's Lynn, introducing a DMU connection at Cambridge for the Fenland area; the King's Cross-Cambridge EMU service will be extended to King's Lynn in May 1991. Provincial Sector also ceased use of Birmingham RC&W Class 104 DMUs at the end of May from North West England. Two twin-sets went to Railway Technical Centre (RTC), Derby, for TCA development work, one of the

sets being due for sale to the Severn Valley Railway (asbestos regulations permitting) when released. Network SouthEast continues to use these units on its Gospel Oak-Barking link but the last intermediate trailers of this Class and their sister Class 110 were withdrawn by the end of September.

A move that really caused some surprise was the decision of Parcels Sector to cease use of DMUs at the end of September. Five BR Derby Class 114/1 converted two-car units and five purpose-built Gloucester RC&W Class 128 single cars were made surplus. Building dates of 1956 and 1959 respectively belie the fact that the former had all been rebuilt over the previous three years with roller shutter doors and the power cars re-engined, and four of the five Class 128s had also been fitted with the Leyland TL11 engine. In fact the trains had one very short reprieve during the second week of October when a special afternoon post and parcels service ran from Chester to St Pancras due to major engineering work at Willesden restricting services to and from Euston. On paper, 14 vehicles were reallocated to Provincial at Chester.

Electrification of the Eastleigh-Portsmouth-Southampton routes in May led to the demise of further Diesel-Electric Multiple Units. Included was the last Class 203 Hastings gauge unit, latterly reduced to four-cars as Unit No 203001 and operating the Ashford-Hastings line. This was subsequently sent to Ilford depot where conversion work for de-icing was carried out. Other routes at present worked by DEMUs are Salisbury-Basingstoke-Reading, East Croydon-Uckfield, and Clapham Junction-Kensington Olympia. All four routes are being reviewed for electrification.

Left:
An unusual view of Waterloo station on 21 August, with Class 455 EMUs seen in profusion for the evening suburban rush hour services, and Class 455/9 No 5906 departing as the 17.20 for Dorking. All sliding-door stock on NSE now displays Sector livery, the final one having been painted at Selhurst in June.

Below:
With electricity switched out between Euston and Tring as a result of engineer's possession on the early part of Sunday morning, 17 June, incoming and outgoing trains were required to utilise diesel power. In lieu of the usual Class 321/4 EMU, the 06.49 Northampton-Euston service is formed of two Bletchley-based Class 108 DMUs led by DMC No 54194, here approaching Queen's Park, near the end of the journey.

Bottom:
The 17.30 Waterloo-Bournemouth train passes Raynes Park at speed on 30 April formed of Class 73/1 No 73130 *City of Portsmouth* leading a 3REP and a pair of 4TCs.

Left:
Forming a special working in connection with the naming of Class 73/1 No 73112 (see page 15), an immaculate Class 411/5 4CEP unit No 1545 passes beneath Canterbury West signalbox on 3 April and enters the station.

Below:
Forming the 06.38 Weymouth/06.55 Parkestone-Waterloo service, Class 442 'Wessex Electrics' Nos 2422/2417 pass through Surbiton station on 21 August, with Class 423/0 4VEP No 3068 proceeding in the opposite direction.

Bottom:
With Marylebone out of use for resignalling for two weeks in September, a revised service on the Chiltern Lines was diverted to and from Paddington. On 22 September, a hybrid six-car DMU forms the 10.29 Paddington-Aylesbury train passing Greenford signalbox, led by BR Derby-built Class-115 DMBS No 51894.

5
The Stourbridge Extension

John Whitehouse and Geoff Dowling

After years of stagnation, cutbacks and closures the railways of Birmingham and the West Midlands are enjoying a series of reopenings and new initiatives. The local passenger transport authority, now known as Centro, has always been pro-rail and instrumental in developing the now famous Birmingham Cross City line from Lichfield to Redditch.

Whilst of late this line has experienced problems due to worn out equipment, an electrification scheme is now in progress: civil engineering work has just commenced together with an order being placed for 18 new Class 323 electric multiple units which will operate the service.

Centro was also involved in the reopening of the passenger service north of Walsall to Hednesford, in conjunction with British Rail and Staffordshire County Council. Hopefully, this service will eventually continue to Rugeley and make a connection with the West Coast main line. The reopening involved capital expenditure on new stations at Bloxwich, Broad Lane, Landywood, Cannock and Hednesford itself. Additionally, a new station has been provided at Tame Bridge between Bescot and Hamstead which acknowledges the passenger growth potential between Walsall and Birmingham.

The reopening of Snow Hill Station in October 1987 was, perhaps, the most symbolic act. Located on the very same site as its illustrious predecessor, the new station has re-established the railway presence and opened the city's financial quarter to the rail-

Above left:
At Langley Green goods yard, the remains of life-expired manual signalling lies on the ground as Class 156 Super Sprinter No 156409 heads for Birmingham New Street forming the 14.27 service from Great Malvern on 15 August. Skulking behind the bushes is Class 37/0 No 37198 waiting to enter the plant of BIP Ltd. *Geoff Dowling*

Left:
Class 150/1 Sprinter No 150127 makes the prescribed stop at the extensively rebuilt Cradeley Heath station on 8 July forming the 09.18 train from Kidderminster to Birmingham New Street. On the opposite platform stands the new remote control cameras that would shortly be controlling the level crossing immediately north of the station. *Geoff Dowling*

50

way commuter. It is a northern terminus for the south of city routes from Leamington, Solihull and Stratford Upon Avon. As a consequence, the terminus at Moor Street was closed, being replaced by a new through station.

However, this only tells half the story: the new Snow Hill was not planned as a terminus, as the trackbed of the ex-Great Western main line through Handsworth and West Bromwich to Wolverhampton had been purposely kept virtually intact.

A second cross-city line has long been talked of, and a decision by early 1991 confirming the go ahead from the Department of Transport is confidently expected. A through Solihull to Stourbridge line is planned, linking Snow Hill with the existing route at Smethwick West.

Smethwick West to Stourbridge is known as 'The Stourbridge Extension'. The name reflects the history of the line: the first railway to Stourbridge was from Oxford via Worcester to Wolverhampton, taking its name from these three locations, but known locally as 'the Old Worse and Worse' reflecting its operations at the time. In 1860, a railway was commenced from Stourbridge towards Old Hill. The Stourbridge Railway, as it was then called obtained authorisation in 1861 to continue to Smethwick and the line was opened throughout in 1867 by which time the new through route had been absorbed into the Great Western Railway.

Not only did the new line join the Great Western Birmingham to Wolverhampton main line at Handsworth, but also the rival London and North Western Stour Valley route at Galton Junction. However, the latter connection did not assume any importance until the actual closure of the original Snow Hill station, when Extension Line trains were diverted into Birmingham New Street.

The Stourbridge Extension today has stations located at Stourbridge Junction, (so named as a branch diverges to Stourbridge Town, which was a separate railway opened in 1879), Lye, Cradley Heath, Old Hill, Rowley Regis, Langley Green and Smethwick West. The Great Western influence can still be seen today, despite modernisation, particularly at Smethwick West and Langley Green where the booking halls are unmistakably of that company's origin. Cradley Heath has been totally rebuilt, once having had staggered platforms on either side of a level crossing. Now, it is a bus and train interchange station with spacious booking hall and waiting room with a new platform on the Down-side adjacent to the Up. At Rowley Regis, the booking hall and main waiting room straddle the track at road level, but the rather spartan platform canopies spoil the overall image. Lye and Old Hill have basic facilities and shelters only. From the commencement of the 1990 summer timetable the basic service pattern consisted of an all-station service to Stourbridge Junction over 30min, with a fast service stopping only at Cradley Heath, also every half hour and continuing to Worcester or Hereford.

The trains are well used and patronage has been rising steadily over the past few years. A combination of frequent and convenient trains, with bus interchange points and ample car parking space at a time of growing road congestion, are the main factors.

However, as with the Lichfield to Redditch line, unreliability of life-expired diesel multiple-units is now causing some concern. The introduction of Class 150 Sprinters has helped, but they are not totally suitable for the heavy loadings which occur in the morning and evening rush hour. The allocated Class 150 sets are being refurbished, involving new seating arrangements which will go some way to alleviating the over crowding problem.

The only other passenger trains which can be seen are diverted expresses to and from the south on Sundays. Indeed, the past two summer timetables have seen expresses booked via Stourbridge, albeit non-stop. Some call at Worcester and Kidderminster (for the Severn Valley Railway) bringing an element of variety to the line. Additionally, engineering possessions on the Lickey route necessitate diversions via Stourbridge. Traction nowadays is restricted to IC125 units and Class 47s, although until recently Class 45s and Class 50s were regular visitors.

Freight is sparse: there is a rail-connected oil terminal at Rowley Regis but this sees little rail activity. A sizeable freight yard exists at Langley Green, from which a daily trip working from Bescot carries chemicals to the works of Albright and Wilson, located on the truncated remains of the ex-Oldbury branch which diverges at Langley Green. This trip also services Handsworth Cement Sidings and a scrapyard, both of which are situated alongside the Old Great Western line from Snow Hill.

Additionally, a company train from Earles Sidings, on the Hope Valley Line, also serves Handsworth, arriving in the late evenings. Locomotives to be seen on the branch to

Below:

Near the entrance of the 896yd long tunnel between Rowley Regis and Old Hill stations, long-range fuel tank (ILRA) Class 47/4 No 47807 threads between old and new signalling on 29 July, hauling the 08.55 Sundays only Wolverhampton-Exeter St Davids train. *Geoff Dowling*

Handsworth vary between Classes 31, 37 and 47.

Until recently, the extension was known for its manual signalling with boxes located at Smethwick Junction (by Smethwick West), Langley Green, Rowley Regis, Cradley Heath and Stourbridge Junction. Rowley Regis was virtually permanently switched out due to little traffic for the adjacent oil terminal. Signalling was a mixture of upper and lower quadrant semaphore and colour-light.

In March 1989 a £2.2 million resignalling scheme was commenced to abolish the manual signalling and introduce a new panel at Stourbridge Junction to control the whole route. On 12 August 1990 the new system was commissioned, fringe signalboxes now being at Blakedown to the south and New Street Panel from Galton Junction. The benefits will be to increase the number of paths available which is vital for the future success of the route and to improve train regulation. Within the resignalling there exists a facility to add on the Snow Hill extension at the appropriate time.

The future for the 'Stourbridge Extension' is exciting: the re-connection with Snow Hill will bring all the benefits of the second Cross City route for which the preparations are at an advanced stage. Additionally, new stations are planned at Galton Bridge, to replace Smethwick West and form an interchange with the Birmingham to Wolverhampton Stour Valley route, Halfords Lane which will be an interchange with the proposed Midland Metro and also serve the nearby West Bromwich Albion football ground and the Jewellery Quarter, which is an area of Birmingham presently undergoing rapid regeneration.

At Langley Green, the remaining section of the Oldbury branch serves Albright & Wilsons chemical plant, and until the signalbox closed, the branch was entered by means of a token obtained from the signalman. The crew of Class 31/1 No 31146 await the token before their afternoon trip freight down to the plant. *Geoff Dowling*

On 15 August, Class 37/0 No 37198 takes the right-hand curve at Smethwick West, leading to Galton Junction, hauling 7T48, a trip working from Langley Green yard to Bescot. *Geoff Dowling*

The Midland Metro will run alongside the British Rail Line from Snow Hill to Halfords Lane, making the intermediate stops and acting as a feeder service thus greatly enhancing the number of journey options available.

An unrelated spin-off will be to relieve the pressure at New Street station, which is now working at full capacity.

It is hoped that work will commence in 1991 for a completion by May 1994.

Thanks are due to John Dawson of British Rail in Birmingham and Malcolm Keeley of Centro for their help in preparing this article.

Above:
Tyseley-based DMU set No T342, formed of a Class 115 trailer No 59673 sandwiched between a pair of Class 116 DMBSs Nos 53055/56, and since disbanded, approaches Smethwick West station, while Class 37/0 No 37198 awaits the road to Langley Green with a haul of scrap metal from Coopers metals, and cement empties from Handsworth terminal. *John Whitehouse*

Above:
Working a Pathfinder Tours 'Gloucester 150' Open Day special from Birmingham New Street, Class 56 No 56034 passes Stourbridge Junction signalbox, which has now been refitted as a power box and controls the Stourbridge extension line. *John Whitehouse*

A view from the past. On 19 September 1986, Class 25/1 No 25057 has just crossed over the Stour Valley line en route to Handsworth cement terminal. As mentioned in this article, providing 'Centro's' proposals are approved, Galton Bridge station will be located at this point. *John Whitehouse*

The ex-Rowley Regis signalbox dated back to 1887, but the advent of multiple signalling, which was completed in August 1990, brought about its demise, together with the fine selection of semaphore signals it once controlled. Hauling the 07.20 InterCity train from Manchester Piccadilly to Poole, ILRA Class 47/4 No 47824 Glorious Devon speeds by. *John Whitehouse*

Left:

Class 150/1 Sprinter No 150127 restarts the 09.18 Kidderminster-Birmingham New Street train from Rowley Regis station on 8 July. Calling only at Stourbridge Junction, Cradeley Heath and Rowley Regis, arrival time at New Street station is scheduled for 09.50. *John Whitehouse*

Left:

Another Intercity long-range fuel tank Class 47/4, No 47826 *Thomas Telford*, passes the remaining bracket signal at Cradeley Heath on 24 June, powering the 08.55 Wolverhampton-Exeter St Davids InterCity train. *John Whitehouse*

Below:

Tyseley-based DMU set No T337, formed of Class 116 DMBSs Nos 53853 and 53838 together with Class 115 TS No 59751, is stabled at temporary buffer-stops in Birmingham Snow Hill station on a warm day in March, awaiting the evening commuter rush. The new Snow Hill station was designed as a through station, and current proposals for a second cross-city route will see a new line constructed on the old trackbed, which has been retained more or less intact through Handsworth and West Bromwich to Wolverhampton. *John Whitehouse*

6

Seaside Summer Saturdays

Brian Beer

It is 06.30 on a Saturday morning in August as the sun shows signs of breaking through the clouds over Aberystwyth. A bleary-eyed camera-laden enthusiast emerges from the Cambrian Hotel opposite the railway station, cursing the vagaries of the timetable which dictate that the only locomotive-hauled departure of the day will be at 07.08! Once on the platform, eyes are turned expectantly in the direction of Machynlleth, to await the arrival of the train which will form the only departure of the day to London. Because radio signalling is used on the line, an appropriately-equipped member of the PCFA (Provincial, Cardiff) Pool is confidently anticipated. No 37430 *Cwmbran* eventually appears, on paper part of the FPBC Pool for use on Stanlow petroleum traffic, but in practice part of Provincial's resources. Several frames are exposed during the run-round procedure, with the pink-tinged dawn sky forming the backdrop, and several more as the train belatedly departs. Summer Saturday on the Cambrian has begun.

The other terminus on the Cambrian coast, at Pwllheli, also receives locomotive-hauled trains, with two workings in and out, the 22.50 (Friday) from Euston, which returns as the 'Snowdonian' at 09.32, and the 09.03 ex-Euston, which returns at 16.56. The latter two workings utilise the locomotive from the 07.08 from Aberystwyth, and thus only two different machines can actually be seen, but the shortfall in quantity is more than compensated for by the superb scenery in the area, with the bridge over the Mawddach estuary at Barmouth being just one of the many excellent locations for the photographer. These particular workings use motive power dedicated to passenger work, but this is by no means the story at other coastal resorts.

Railfreight Rarities

Since the advent of sectorisation on British Rail, many locomotives have become rare performers on passenger trains, which have been almost solely the preserve of ETH-fitted machines allocated to the passenger sectors. Some opportunities for photographers and those interested in haulage by Railfreight motive power do occur as a result of short-notice substitutions due to locomotive failures, which, though fairly frequent, are difficult to predict. However, on summer Saturdays, the situation changes dramatically, with freight sub-Sectors making their traction available for passenger train haulage, thereby providing an opportunity for the enthusiast to combine rare motive power on interesting lines with fish and chips and candy floss, on a day trip to the coast. At the same time, other holiday locations normally served only by DMUs see an influx of locomotive-hauled trains and other types of motive power, making them well worth a visit.

Below:
With headlight and marker lights aglow, 'Mainline'-liveried Class 37/4 No 37430 *Cwmbran* **prepares to leave Aberystwyth on 18 August with the town's sole through working to London, the 07.08 to Euston.** *Brian Beer*

East Anglian Excursions

Great Yarmouth is one of the most popular holiday resorts in the country, and has proved equally interesting for the enthusiast during 1990. The two routes between Norwich and this coastal resort offer a combination of varied traction, semaphore signalling and as many as 10 locomotive-hauled workings in each direction. These are divided more or less evenly between the two routes, and thus pose a problem for the photographer, since it is very difficult to cover all trains, except by taking up position on the trunk section of the route between Norwich and Brundall. From here, the route to Great

Above left:
Class 73/1 electro-diesel No 73109 approaches Hilsea on 28 July heading the 09.15(SO) 'Network Express' from Plymouth to Brighton, having taken over from a Class 50 at Portsmouth Harbour. This locomotive is now painted into NSE livery and named *Battle of Britain 50th Anniversary.*
Brian Beer

Left:
Decked out in full InterCity livery, complete with swallow, ILRA Class 47/4 No 47839 arrives at Eastbourne on 4 August with empty stock to form the 08.55(SO) departure for Glasgow Central. The long-range fuel tanks fitted would probably obviate the need for a change of motive power en route but, in fact, the locomotive is only rostered as far as Birmingham New Street, where electric traction is scheduled to take over. *Brian Beer*

Below:
Rounding the Firsby loop, the 06.27(SO) Leeds-Skegness train is powered by 60mph-limited Class 31/1 No 31522, and passes Tyseley-based DMU set No T314 heading in the opposite direction and forming the 09.44 Skegness-Nottingham service. Pressed Steel Co-built Driving Motors Nos 51348 and 51390 are at each end of Class 115 trailer No 59677. *John C. Baker*

Above:

The unique green-liveried 'Hoover' No 50007 *Sir Edward Elgar* leaves Cosham on 21 July with the 09.15(SO) Plymouth-Brighton train, the locomotive being replaced by Class 73/1 No 73141 at Portsmouth harbour for the final leg of the journey. By tracing the train's movements through BR timetables 123, 135 and 186, one can eventually discover that with scheduled stops at Newton Abbot, Teignmouth, Dawlish, Dawlish Warren, Exeter St Davids, Salisbury, Southampton, Fareham, Cosham, Portsmouth Harbour (reverse), Portsmouth & Southsea, Havant, Chichester, Barnham, and Worthing, that the passengers returning from their holidays will eventually arrive at their Brighton destination at 16.03, a total journey time for this unusual service of nearly 7hr. *Brian Beer*

Left:

Class 31/1 No 31165, in an earlier version of Railfreight Sector livery, approaches Great Yarmouth on 30 June with the 07.52 'Holidaymaker Express' from Birmingham New Street, which it took over at Norwich. Both locomotive and the usual motley collection of stock formed the 13.25 return working. *Brian Beer*

Left:

Running 2½hr late, Class 47/0 No 47145 *Merddin Emrys* passes Thetford on 8 September, hauling the 09.37 Leeds-Great Yarmouth train which it took over from a failed locomotive near Sheffield. This Tinsley-based 'Duff' is the pride of the depot, painted in a form of metallic blue, and provided with some special embellishments to include the cast, but unofficial, nameplates. *Antony Guppy*

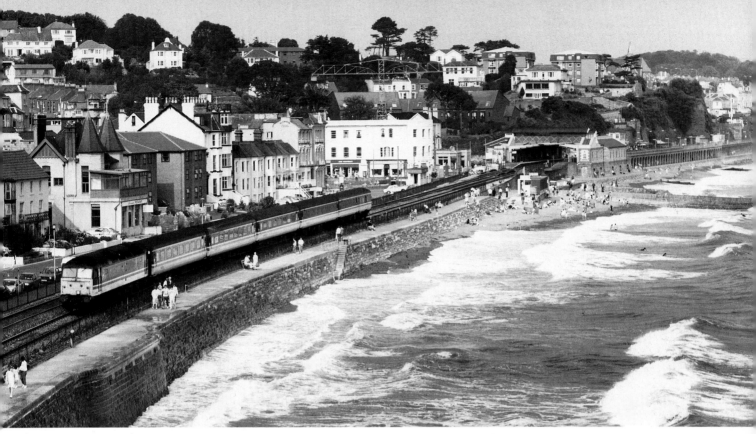

Above:
With the sea at Dawlish looking a mite rough on 15 September, ILRA Class 47/4 No 47804 heads for next stop at Teignmouth, hauling the 09.22 'InterCity Holidaymaker' from Edinburgh to Paignton. *Brian Morrison*

Yarmouth via Acle is single-track, whilst the alternative route continues as double-track to Reedham, thence via the remotely situated diminutive platform at Berney Arms. Locomotive diagramming is of particular interest on these workings, since all trains reverse and change locomotives at Norwich. Motive power arriving from London and the Midlands does not work forward to Great Yarmouth, these 'portions' being booked for haulage in 1990 by four locomotives — one Parcels Class 47 (RXLD), one Departmental Class 31 (DCAA), one Provincial Class 31/4 (PCDB), and a Class 37 from the Stratford Railfreight Construction pool (FAGS). This variety, not only of locomotive types, but also of liveries, together with the many attractive locations on both routes, provide a fascinating day out for the photographer. Reedham, in particular, can be recommended not only for its Great Eastern signalbox, and operational swing bridge on the line to Lowestoft, but also for the hostelry a few yards from the station in which to slake one's thirst between trains!

Along the Sunny South Coast

Although locomotive-hauled trains in the southeast are less numerous than in some areas, there were nevertheless several workings of note in 1990. The 09.05 departure from Brighton offered the opportunity to ride the Sussex Coast behind a Class 73 to Portsmouth Harbour, with the option to continue behind a 'Hoover' to Plymouth. The 09.15 departure from Plymouth to Brighton utilised a second Class 50, but formed part of the same Class 73 diagram forward from Portsmouth Harbour. The section between this location and Portcreek Junction is covered twice by each train, but with different traction, and offers good opportunities for photography, particularly on the bridge across the Broom Channel. To local enthusiasts at Eastbourne, accustomed to a 100%

EMU service, the summer Saturday departures at 08.55 (to Glasgow Central) and 14.10 (to Manchester Piccadilly) behind Class 47s may well be the highlight of the year. The earlier depature certainly offers entertainment for the onlooker, if only because of the complicated propelling movements to and from the carriage sidings which are required for the locomotive to run round, due to the failure to diagram a second locomotive to assist. This working is booked for a member of the ILRA (Inter City, long range fuel) Pool, based at Bristol Bath Road, and is only one of a number of seaside visits made by the ILRA Class 47/4 variants.

Have fuel, will travel

The fitting of long-range fuel tanks to 53 examples of Class 47 in recent years has ensured that these particular machines are seen across the entire network. Saturday diagrams in 1990 have taken them to such diverse locations as Penzance, Blackpool, Tenby, Poole, Weymouth and Dover. Unfortunately, the class does seem to have an 'image problem', being regarded by many people as uninteresting. This is perhaps a little unfair, if only because of the wide variation of liveries that the 'Duffs' carry. Anyway, to those used only to CIGs and VEPs, even a 47 may have some appeal — all things are relative!

What no Choppers?

Countless thousands of additional visitors to the East Coast resort of Skegness during the 1980s were generated by excursions from the Midlands which offered haulage behind pairs

of Class 20s. However, Saturdays in 1990 did not produce the hoped-for sight of the 30-year-old English Railfreight machines trundling to the Lincolnshire coast, with Classes 47/4 (Parcels Sector) and 31/4 being the scheduled performers. Although the line itself is still largely controlled by mechanical signalling, it is rather featureless otherwise, and its attraction has always depended largely on the motive power visiting the resort. The only saving grace in 1990 has been the mid-week relief trains, which have seen Class 20s on occasions. Is it too much to hope that Regional Railways will decide to boost its summer Saturday revenue in 1990 and re-instate what has become an institution? The continuing popularity of the 'Choppers' has again been demonstrated on occasional outings north of the Border.

Unadvertised but well publicised

For variety and unpredictability, the train of 1990 was almost certainly the 10.40 Ayr to Carlisle and return. In addition to Class 20s, the working also produced 26005 (FEPE — Lothian's Coal!) on 11 August, and 31412 of Crewe DMD on 15 September. On other occasions, the traction tended to be Class 37s taking a break from their normal Coal traffic duties. As a result, although not advertised in the Public Timetable, this working was invariably well-filled with enthusiasts, demonstrating the efficiency of the 'Gricer's Grapevine' as well as the revenue-earning potential of certain types of power.

Way Down West

Diagrammed workings in Devon and Cornwall promised little variety, with Class 47/4s being the only visitors — on paper — following the loss of Old Oak Common's allocation of 'Hoovers' in July, which until that time had performed fairly consistently on the 08.02 Paddington to Paignton and 13.24 return. However, the most interesting aspect

Above:

Two return locomotive-hauled trips between Shrewsbury and Pwllheli were scheduled for the duration of the summer timetable. In this view, Class 37/4 No 37430 *Cwmbran* leaves the Fairbourne stop with the second south-bound working, the 16.56 Pwllheli-Euston on 18 August. *Brian Beer*

Left:

With 'Hoovers' now rare west of Exeter, one train that could almost be relied upon to produce one during the summer months was the 09.05(SO) Brighton-Plymouth 'Network Express', the return journey of which is referred to on page 58. Restarting the train from Dawlish on 15 September, is No 50008 *Resolution*. *Brian Morrison*

Below:

But for the give-way locomotive headlight, this view of a Class 37 in BR 'corporate blue' livery hauling an all-matching rake of blue/grey Mk 2 stock through Brundall, could almost have been taken in the mid-1970s. Roaring through the station to make up lost time on a 20min deficit with the 09.37 Leeds-Yarmouth train, Class 37/1 No 37219 was actually photographed on 21 July 1990. *Antony Guppy*

of railway operating is often the difference between theory and practice. With extremely hot weather conditions prevailing, and a pool of assorted locomotives available to assist failures, many holidaymakers found themselves enjoying unusual traction on trains to Paignton, Penzance, and even Newquay on occasions. With the imminent demise of the DCWA pool of 'Hoovers' being predicted, it is unlikely that the class will be seen in any great numbers in future years in the West Country, and 1990 may well be viewed as the Indian summer of the class.

Nevertheless, let us hope that the sight and sound of unusual motive power on loco-motive-hauled passenger trains throughout the country will continue to form part of the summer Saturday scene for many years — a 10-coach 'Sprinter' won't have the same appeal, somehow.

7

North Wales in 1990

A. Wyn Hobson

1990 saw the motive power situation on BR's North Wales main line and its branches suspended between two eras. The bulk of local and semi-fast passenger traffic was still shared between 30-year-old Class 101 and 108 diesel multiple-units, on the one hand, and Class 142 Pacer and 150/1 and 150/2 Sprinter units on the other. Class 155s had returned to the workings to and from Cardiff in 1989, but May 1990 saw the disappearance of the few Class 156 workings to and from the North East, as well as the withdrawal of the last Class 104 units from Chester depot. Meanwhile, Class 117s continued to appear in North Wales on a few diagrams originating at Derby, and Tyseley Class 116s continued to work the Blaenau Ffestiniog branch, in the absence of any long-term solution to the problem of excessive flange-wear and noise that had put a summary end to the use of Sprinters and Pacers on the branch in the mid-1980s.

DVTs had begun appearing on a few Euston-Holyhead expresses in 1989, but remained dead loads on the Crewe-Holyhead section, as they could not be operated in conjunction with the Class 47s that remained the line's staple express passenger power. Class 31s became a little more numerous on lesser passenger workings, due to the shortage of Sprinters that affected several parts of BR at that time; the summer timetable saw a dated Monday-Friday Manchester-Llandudno return diagram operated by a Class 31 and three or four coaches (a modified version of a diagram also operated in the summer of 1989, but this time not filling in with a trip down the Blaenau Ffestiniog branch), and several Class 31-hauled Saturday workings between North Wales and Liverpool or Manchester. As well as the Class 31/1s and 31/4s that might have been expected, these workings not infrequently produced Class 31/5 locomotives, recently modified and reliveried for use by the Civil Engineer's department.

On the freight side, the Speedlink workings (never extensive) seemed to be partaking of the general decline in such traffic, and the much-mooted scheme to open a timber siding at Roman Bridge, on the Blaenau Ffestiniog branch, came to naught. The late afternoon Freightliner workings from Trafford Park and Lawley Street to Holyhead were retimed to run at night, but during 1990 an early afternoon down Freightliner working was inserted into the timetable on an 'as required' basis — and, by the end of summer, appeared to be required most days, and to be getting longer! The daily working to and from Point of Ayr Colliery, using a pair of Class 20s, and the twice-weekly

nuclear flask trains from Trawsfynydd, generally behind a Class 31, continued; but the only traffic that could be said to be flourishing was the stone and ballast trains — sometimes three or four in a day — from the ARC terminal at Penmaenmawr, on which Class 47 and 31 locomotives predominated, with very occasional appearances by Class 37s.

The Class 158 Express Sprinter modified for clearance-testing ran to Holyhead on 8 August; but as the year drew to its close, the long-promised introduction of these units to North Wales passenger services still appeared a distant prospect. There was talk of the introduction of HSTs on the London expresses the following summer, and of their diversion down the Midland Main Line to St Pancras (or was it to be King's Cross? It depended which journalist you were listening to). And local politicians still called — as they had done for at least 20 years, especially during run-ups to elections — for electrification of the North Wales Main Line, on the grounds of its being the main transport artery to Ireland. Another such proposal, to rebuild the long-closed Menai Bridge-Caernarfon branch, caused a brief flutter locally during the year, and died the death. Meanwhile, on the railway itself — as on many other parts of BR, in that year of deepening financial and motive power crisis — the sense was of a holding on through an enforced pause, as the system waited for the arrival of a future in which further contraction or major developments seemed equal possibilities.

Hauling a Mk 3 DVT and all-matching InterCity Sector Mk 2 stock, green Class 47/4 No 47500 *Great Western* heads the Sunday 13.00 Holyhead-Euston service through Penmaenmawr on 15 July. On the mountainside, work is commencing on a new hard rock tunnel to carry part of the A99 'Expressway'; the town bypass section (right foreground) had been opened the previous winter. *Great Western* was a regular performer on the North Wales main line at this time. *Wyn Hobson*

Right:
**Class 142 'Pacer' No 142051 forms the Sunday
13.30 Llandudno Junction-Holyhead local service
on 15 July, and climbs away from mist-
enshrouded Penmaenmawr towards the next
scheduled stop at Llanfairfechan.** *Wyn Hobson*

Below:
**On 1 August, Class 47/4 No 47425 Holbeck heads
a Holyhead-bound Freightliner through Ty Croes
and passes the old LNWR signalbox there which
dates from 1871. Unfortunately, all is not as it
appears, as the structure is now just a crossing
box, its electrics having been condemned in
February 1989, creating a long block section
between Valley and Gaerwen, which can cause
long delays for some services when there is a
late-running train in front of them.** *Wyn Hobson*

Above:

One of North Wales's few remaining industrial landscapes provides a backcloth to the 09.44 Manchester Victoria-Llandudno train passing Point of Ayr Colliery, Talacre, on 8 August. Powering mainly NSE-liveries stock is Class 31/1 No 31248, one of the Departmental stock of Civil Engineer's locomotives based at Crewe (DCMC Pool). *Wyn Hobson*

Left:

Led by a Tyseley-based Class 116 DMBS, unit No T327 arrives at Gogledd Llanrwst/Llanrwst North on 16 June, forming the 09.36 service from Blaneau Ffestiniog to Llandudno. Llanrwst North has the only remaining passing loop on the branch. The run-down state of the now unstaffed station is evident; the new Llanrwst station, opened a quarter of a mile down the line less than a year previously, had already been subjected to extensive vandalism. *Wyn Hobson*

Left:

Probably on its way to load ballast at Penmaenmawr Quarry, Class 31/1 No 31158 passes the classic location of Conwy Castle with an engineer's train on 25 July. *Wyn Hobson*

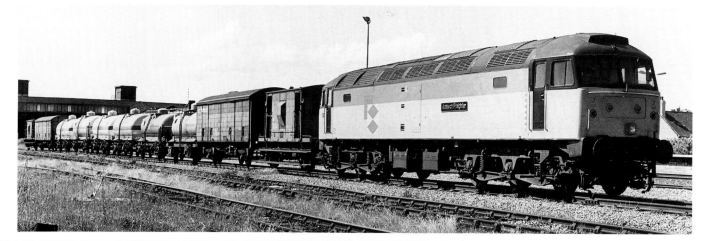

8
Picture Parade

Above:

On 25 November, a much-maligned but very reliable 4EPB EMU passes engineers at work on a bridge spanning one of the many roads in southeast London, over which the railway passes between London Bridge and New Cross. With the modern City skyline as a background, Class 415/4 No 5475 forms the 12.53 train from Charing Cross to Hayes, in Kent. Using a Nikon FE2 camera with 85mm lens, the exposure of Kodak Ektachrome 64 film was 1/500 sec @ f3.5. *Brian Morrsion*

Left:

Heading south, Class 37/7 No 37718 approaches Leicester station on 19 December with a haul of empty scrap metal wagons returning to Cardiff. Ektachrome 64 film was again used in a Nikon FE2 camera fitted with an 85mm lens; exposure 1/250sec @ f5.6 on automatic mode. *Brian Morrison*

65

Facing page, top:
The view through the windscreen of a Class 43 HST powercar at speed near Didcot on 29 March, as a Departmental grey-liveried Class 31/4 No 31417 hauls a recalcitrant Class 47/4 back to Bristol Bath Road depot for attention following failure. Using a 24mm wide-angle lens on a Nikon FM2 camera, the exposure to successfully stop movement at a closing speed of over 150mph was 1/4000sec @ f2.8 on Ilford XP1 film rated at 400ASA. *Brian Morrison*

Facing page, bottom:
On 8 November, the 1,000th train of concrete segments for the Channel Tunnel departed from the TML site on the Isle of Grain and headed for the Shakespeare Cliff site, hauled by Class 33/0s Nos 33021 and 33051 *Shakespeare Cliff*, both in Railfreight Construction livery. A Nikon FM2 camera fitted with a 135mm telephoto lens was used for this result with XP1 film rated at 400ASA; exposure for a cloudy day was 1/250sec @ f6.3. *Brian Morrison*

Left:
Utilising a variety of motive power, to include Class 20s and Class 73s on diesel power, the Cambridge Gala Day on 29 September was adjudged a considerable success, despite the rain which came down heavily for most of the day. With Class 310 EMU No 310049 in use as coaching stock, a pair of electro-diesels, Nos 73103 and 73129, approach Ely North Junction with the 09.30 'Fenman' special from Cambridge to King's Lynn. With Kodak Tri-X film rated at 400ASA in a Pentax 6x7 camera, the exposure on a standard lens to retain depth of field at a maximum, was 1/250sec @ f6.3. *John C. Baker*

Below:
The wild uplands of Maesteg in South Wales. Looking quite incongruous on the sinuous track, is Railfreight Coal sector-liveried Class 37/5 No 37698 Coedbach, with a haul of old vacuum-braked MDV wagons in tow. The train is leaving Maesteg washery, and will have to reverse before travelling via Tondu. Using a Nikon 301 camera with 105mm lens and 400ASA XP1 film, the exposure was 1/250sec @ f6.3. *John Vaughan*

9

The Jacob Syndrome - BR's Coats of many colours

Brian Morrison

All photographs by the author unless otherwise credited

Once upon a time, the moguls of British Rail decreed that all locomotives would be panted in a plain blue hue, relieved only by a full yellow front end. Suburban multiple units and coaching stock would match, and only mainline coaching stock would deviate a little by having two-tone blue and grey. Today a plain blue locomotiive is becoming a rare sight, and plain blue coaches in passenger service are non-existent.

I suppose it all started when the Class 50s were given a very large BR logo and TOPS number — quite eye-opening at the time, but with the welter of colour which now exists throughout the country, quite nondescript today. With the advent of Sectorisation, it was intended that there would be five basic liveries for InterCity, Railfreight, Network SouthEast, Regional Railways and Parcels. In fact, due to changes which have come about as a result of aesthetics, weathering problems and changes of mind, InterCity now has its attractive 'swallow' livery, but motive power and coaching stock still exist in the Sector's old colours, and is often mixed together with unfortunate results. RailFreight Sector commenced with a grey

Below:

On 26 April, Departmental 'general-user'-liveried Class 47/3 No 47343 shunts the Workington-Willesden freight at Corkickle, on the Cumbrian coast line. Looking reasonable when clean, the drab grey paintwork becomes very drab indeed when work stained, and is considered as the least successful of the variety of liveries which have been introduced on BR over the past few years. In contrast, Class 31/1 No 31275 is dressed up in attractive Railfreight Sector two-tone grey with Coal sub-Sector decals, and waits on the main line to provide transport back to Workington for the shunting staff. *Dave McAlone*

livery, added a red sole-bar to later examples, and finished with a two-tone grey with no fewer than six sub-Sector decals of varying colour and design. Network SouthEast's red, white, blue and grey, at first appeared startling and most 'un-British', but has now been accepted as normal throughout the Sector; only the older slam-door stock, which is awaiting replacement, remaining in blue and grey, having been repainted from plain blue after the blue and grey ceased to be used for express stock. The original NSE blue has been superseded by a darker version, however, and the 'Wessex Electrics', Classes 321 and 456 and the 'new' Isle of Wight stock all have their own special livery styles incorporating the same colours. Before Provincial Sector was renamed Regional Railways, it had two basic liveries, the original light blue with a dark blue band, and the second, turning the colours upside-down, with a dark blue top and light blue band. Again the types get mixed up and look any-

Right:

With Regions phased out in favour of Sectors, the ex-Class 6B Hastings Buffet Car No 60755, which had been in use as the Southern Region General Manager's Saloon No TDB975025 since conversion in 1969, is now owned by Network SouthEast Departmental and, towards the end of the year, was duly painted at Selhurst Depot into Sector colours. The attractive coach is seen here on display at Stewarts Lane Depot in company with matching Class 73/1 No 73109 *Battle of Britain 50th Anniversary*.

Below:

Inside Eastleigh Works on 22 November, Class 150/1 Sprinter No 150112 receives modifications, and has been painted from its original Provincial Sector colours into the distinctive livery of West Midlands 'Centro'

Right:

Displaying the 'Express' livery of Regional Railways, Class 158 unit No 158732 stands outside the Works buildings of BREL Derby Litchurch Lane, following completion on 24 September.

thing but corporate to the onlooker. A third livery of light fawn with black window surround and light and dark blue stripes has now appeared for the Class 158 Provincial Express but Provincial Scotrail have lost their distinctive colours following elimination of locomotive-hauled trains within Scottish Region; it is hoped that Regional Railways refrain from thinking up yet another new livery just because they have changed their title. An individual livery for Parcels Sector has been a fairly recent innovation, and distinctive it is too, with their coaching stock painted red with yellow lining and their locomotives painted red and dark grey.

In addition to this little lot, there is the green and cream West Highland coaching stock, Departmental general-user (or 'orphans') drab and un-lined overall grey for motive power not specifically allocated to any

Above:
Wearing British Airport Authority colours of grey with a green stripe, Class 322 'Stansted Express' EMU No 322483 awaits departure from Liverpool Street station on 7 December forming the 18.35 train to Cambridge. The five units of Class 322 were used on these workings prior to the official opening of Stansted Airport on 15 March 1991.

Left:
Passing March East Junction signalbox on 14 October 1989, Class 47/4 No 47603 *County of Somerset*, in what has become known as 'large loco' livery, drags Class 91 No 91002, in the latest InterCity Sector livery, with the 16.10 train from King's Cross to Leeds. Diesel haulage between Cambridge and Peterborough was necessary due to engineer's line occupation between Huntingdon and Peterborough, services being diverted at Hitchin.

Left:
Four old Class 302 EMUs have been converted for Parcels Sector use and painted into red livery with yellow lining. Classified 302/1, unit No 302991 is loaded with mail at Liverpool Street station on 7 December, from where it will travel to Southend Victoria.

Right:

Providing the unusual sight of a Provincial 'Midline'-liveried unit south of Milton Keynes, Class 310/1 No 310102 formed the 06.54 Walsall-Milton Keynes service on 30 March, which then left its destination, bound for servicing at Bletchley Depot.

Below:

Two eth-fitted Class 31/4s, Nos 31423 Jerome K. Jerome and 31434, hammer through Brandon on 4 August, powering the 10.40(SO) Great Yarmouth-Birmingham New Street train of returning holidaymakers. The leading locomotive is one of only two of the type to have been painted into 'mainline' livery; the train locomotive is still in basic BR 'corporate blue', first introduced in the 1960s. *John C. Baker*

Bottom:

Another new livery appeared on BR during the year, when the four ARC Ltd Class 59/1s arrived from General Motors USA, painted in ARC yellow with grey cabs. On 8 November, No 59103 is on Hither Green Depot alongside Class 33/0 'Crompton' No 33048.

one sector, and that same livery augmented with a yellow upper band for Civil Engineer's stock, and tagged 'Dutch' due to its similarity with Netherlands Railways colours; and one must not overlook InterCity paintwork without the swallow and with the numbers in a sensible position, and called 'Mainline'.

And that is not all, for the various Passenger Transport Executives who contribute to the costs of their transport system, also demand their own colours. The result is West Yorkshire's original colours of green and white have now been changed to red and cream (and of course both types could be observed for some time), and these units can be seen alongside Greater Manchester orange, the chocolate and cream 'Skippers' which were transferred from Cornwall, Trans-Pennine, Network NorthWest and many special 'one-offs' to include green locomotives and those of BRB Research which are decked out in red and blue or red and cream. Tyne and Wear PTE Pacers are painted yellow, Strathclyde stock is in orange with black window surrounds, West Midlands 'Centro' Sprinters are coming out in green and grey with a blue stripe, and even the five Class 322 Stansted Airport EMUs have their own colour scheme of silver/grey with a green band corresponding with British Airports Authority.

A DMU sports GWR colours and others are in a version of their original 1960s green. In addition to all-over blue and various Sector styles, Class 08 shunters can also be seen in black, red, Great Eastern blue, RFS blue/yellow harlequin, and various shades of green. Two Class 73 electro-diesels are in 'Bluebell' blue, and the Hunslet-Barclay Class 20s are decked out in their owner's own colours, together with Yeoman silver and ARC yellow on these company's respective Class 59s; and the latest 'variation' is for a Class 50 to be repainted into original BR 'corporate blue. Has the wheel at last gone full circle?

Painted in BR Research red and blue, Wickham Laboratory Car No 20 (999507) is seen at Egginton Junction on 26 April, en route from the Research Centre, Mickleover, to the Test Centre at Old Dalby. *Bert Wynn*

Left:
Six 1950s vintage Class 307 EMUs were given an extended lease of life when they were transferred from Great Eastern metals to Neville Hill Depot, to work on West Yorkshire PTE services between Leeds and Doncaster. Newly painted into the red and cream livery of the Passenger Transport Executive, No 307122 was the first of the class to be treated in this way and is seen outside Ilford Depot on 22 June.

Below:
In Greater Manchester PTE's colours of orange and brown, Class 504 EMU No 504460 waits to leave a ramshackle-looking Manchester Victoria station on 27 July, forming the 14.00 service for Bury.

Left:
Yet another new livery introduced during 1990, was Parcels Sector red and dark grey for their locomotive fleet. Inside Stratford Major Depot on 13 July, Class 47/4 No 47501 Craftsman is on jacks, receiving attention to its bogies.

Right:
The 'general-user' grey livery illustrated on page 68, was brightened up on Civil Engineer's locomotives by the addition of a wide yellow upper band, as shown on Class 73/1 No 73133 *The Bluebell Railway* at Selhurst Depot on 6 September. Rather akin to the paintwork seen on locomotives of Netherland Railways, the livery immediately became tagged as 'Dutch'. It is being applied to a wide variety of types, to include Classes 31, 33, 37, 47 and even a solitary 50.

10
Paint Your Wagon

Roger Silsbury MCIT

The question of liveries has long been a topic of deep interest to railway historians and whilst the locomotive has always reigned supreme in detailed consideration, with the passenger carriage running a poor second, other facets of railway livery policy have received scant attention until recently. This article seeks to consider the humble goods wagon as it has traditionally been known, although under more modern terminology it has become a freight vehicle!

Why have a livery anyway? In order to protect a railway vehicle from the elements a coating of some description has always been applied and from the basic necessity to provide such protection, embellishments to form a distinctive livery have evolved. According to contemporary accounts, in contrast to the distinctive and elaborate liveries applied to locomotives and carriages, the Victorian goods wagon seems to have nearly always been painted either a shade of grey, or of red. These two colours derived from the basic materials used in the mixing of paint, white lead or iron oxide, and provided a durable covering which adhered well to the wooden bodies and underframes. Ironwork was often coated in a black japan type of paint. The practice of painting the solebars and headstocks in the main body colour stems from these early days of wooden underframed wagons and was continued even when steel underframes became universal. Whilst the colour was defined by a company in instructions to their works, the actual shade which was eventually applied varied enormously according to the whim of the foreman painter at each site, as paint was mixed from raw ingredients as required and according to materials on hand. Add to this the effects of weathering, especially considering the lengthy periods between repainting, and it is not surprising that a definitive colour shade for each company is impossible. Lettering was not universally applied at first, a cast iron plate being the normal form of identification. Gradually, painted identification appeared, and the so-called 'illiterate symbols' adopted by several companies may be considered the first form of corporate livery to appear on goods wagons. Others applied an abbreviated form of the company name, usually as initials in relatively small characters, and it was not until the 1880s that large letters appeared, starting with the Midland Railway. Irrespective of body colour, lettering has been almost exclusively white. Exceptions to the 'all grey or red' were made in the case of a few specialist wagons, eg perishable vans, where a light body colour also necessitated the use of dark lettering.

In contrast to the relatively drab appearance of railway-owned wagons, those owned by private companies were often quite striking in their livery. While the choice of main body colour was dictated by similar considerations to that which faced the railway companies, the private owners were generally quick to appreciate the considerable advertising effect that could be gained by bold, bright lettering and the vast majority applied quite elaborate styles, often with contrast shading adding to the overall effect.

Following the grouping little general change seems to have taken place, each of the major companies following the pattern of the dominant partner of the constituents. Lettering became more elaborate, but always associated with instructions regarding operation of equipment or routeing of the wagon rather than any conscious effort at advertising. This latter did not come about until the advent of containerisation, when it was appreciated that because the containers often found their way into very public places, they were ideal for promoting the company's services; probably the 'Door to Door without handling' slogan and the inclusive furniture removal/travel facilities were the most prominent.

Although some changes in livery of goods wagons were introduced during the 1930s the advent of the Second World War brought an abrupt halt to further development, the scarcity of raw materials causing a retrenchment of practice to the point where only fitted stock, covered unfitted and all steel-bodied stock received an all-over coat of paint, non-fitted open stock having all woodwork left bare apart from patches for essential lettering. The requisitioning of all the privately owned stock, apart from tank wagons and a few specialist types, spelt the end of the striking liveries of earlier years, and by the end of the war the vast majority of goods wagons were looking decidedly down-at-heel. Postwar shortages did not readily permit an improvement in the situation for some years, although the newly-nationalised British Railways did promote a new corporate standard once materials became available whereby all non-fitted stock was painted light grey and fitted stock a shade described as 'bauxite red', which had a distinctly orange hue. Exceptions were made for insulated vehicles which were painted white and ventilated meat vans which were crimson. The former private owner mineral wagons did not profit from this scheme and many bore faded traces of former owners' names at withdrawal. In 1964 a new livery scheme was introduced; grey remained for unfitted stock, but the 'bauxite red' for fitted stock took on a darker brown shade. White gave way to 'ice blue' for insulated vehicles and crimson had by now disappeared. New lettering styles were also introduced. The introduction of air brake stock saw no changes apart from the 'merry-go-round' coal hoppers which had unpainted, galvanised bodies and Freightliner flats which were initially black, later becoming rail blue. In the mid-1970s, a new image began to appear as BR became more design conscious; new build air brake wagons received a maroon livery, although in the event this proved short-lived and by the end of the decade the bright 'flame red', later designated rail red, and grey livery appeared. This took the form of the ends and the top portion of the side being red, the remainder of the side being grey, although low sided steel carriers were more sensibly all-over red. Ten years later and red has lost favour to yellow for ends only, the whole side of all types becoming a dark grey.

In BR days Engineering Department vehicles began by being unrelieved black, followed by a short period of a mid-red; the 1964 changes saw the introduction of all over olive, although former revenue vehicles transferred to the Departmental fleets were often not repainted. The introduction of red and grey to the revenue fleet was matched by yellow and grey on the Departmental fleet. To assist safety by improving visibility track machines received all-over yellow. The advent of a special fleet of wagons for use in the 'Project Mercury' telecommunications scheme saw them painted a bright blue and subsequently the Signal & Telegraph Department has adopted a red and yellow livery, yellow uppermost.

After nationalisation the private owner fleet consisted largely of tank wagons, painted to indicate the type of commodity being carried; dove grey for Class A liquids and plain black for Class B, chemical and LPG tanks having white with red, later orange, bands, all carrying Company lettering and/or logos. The few non-tank private owner wagons retained a semblance of pre-war individuality but increasing manpower costs in the 1960s led to abandonment of company insignia on nearly all privately owned stock. This period may be considered the nadir of livery for all goods wagons, railway and privately owned.

The 1980s have seen a reawakening awareness of 'image' and corporate identity which, coupled with modern synthetic paints available in a wide range of colours, has led to improved livery styles. The flame red adopted by BR a decade ago, whilst striking when

new, suffers from fading to the extent that some vehicles appear a shade of pink after some years. The BR design panel created a totally new image for Railfreight which was launched at Ripple Lane in October 1987. For freight vehicles a mid-grey was chosen for the main body colour, except where galvanised metal surfaces were left in natural colour, with sector symbols applied in the form of self-adhesive panels. To assist with safety, ends of vehicles are painted yellow, although it is an unfortunate fact of life that the most difficult part of the vehicle to clean is painted the light colour and for livery to portray its designed image it must be kept clean. A much more liberal attitude has been taken with regard to application of individual company liveries, with firms like Plasmor, Kronospan and Allied Steel & Wire sponsoring either total repaints or distinctive lettering. Some of the Engineering Departments have also decided to adopt their own distinctive styles and the CS&TE are now being repainted red and yellow and the Civil Engineer modifying the departmental yellow and grey to include the legend 'Civil Link'; for once the wagons foreshadowed the locomotives in having the yellow upper bodyside subsequently adopted as the so-called 'Dutch' livery for departmental traction.

Above:
British Rail has offered companies the opportunity to sponsor repainting of hired, railway-owned wagons in their own livery, subject to inclusion of BR's own corporate logo. Yorkshire-based concrete block manufacturers, Plasmor Ltd, accepted the opportunity to promote their product by adopting a striking green, orange and white livery for their fleet of hired DBA vehicles, which incorporates the company's name and logo in addition to the BR double arrow symbol. *Roger Silsbury*

It is the private owners who have provided the really colourful scene. The acceptance of 'image' by several of the larger companies saw a concerted effort to clean their wagons, quickly followed by the adoption of some quite striking livery styles or embellishments. Base colours now range right across the spectrum and lettering has increased in size; whilst shading has not generally been incorporated, a range of typefaces, symbols and logos have been used ensuring plenty of variety. Both BP Oil and Shell UK Oil adopted forms of coloured stripes allied with their company logo which also appear on their fleets of road vehicles, although it is the former which has taken first advantage of the relaxation in the regulations regarding the permitted colours for tank wagons conveying petroleum and chemical products to launch a totally new livery around their house colours. In addition to the domestic fleets, increasing numbers of European wagons may now be seen and the opening of the Channel Tunnel will swell such ranks further.

The resurgence of colour to adorn the freight vehicles running on British Rail is most welcome, proclaiming the message that Railfreight is a force to be considered in an increasingly environmentally sensitive world.

Below:
BP Oil were the first of the oil companies to take advantage of the relaxation in requirements for oil and chemical tank liveries. In the environmentally conscious 1990s, BP's green and yellow house colours combine effectively to portray their company image. Vehicles depicted are TEA No BP087566 and TTA No BP060194. *Trevor J. Mann*

11
Titled Trains of 1990

Brian Morrison
All photographs by the author unless otherwise credited

Omitting the many and various passenger trains in British Rail's 1990 summer timetable which use such titles as 'Intercity Holidaymaker', 'Holiday maker Express', 'Network Express', 'Portsmouth Express' and 'Gatwick Express', one is still left with 58 services from the six regions which carry a name — or 56 if 'Dales Rail Service' and 'Heart of Wales Rambler' are deleted as being more a description of their route than a prestige train. Some of the names, such as 'Flying Scotsman', 'Cornish Riviera' and 'Royal Scot', are legendary, while others well known in steam days, faded into obscurity only to be resurrected by the marketing men in these more enlightened times; the likes of 'Royal Wessex', Master Cutler', 'Royal Dutchy', Atlantic Coast Express' and 'Yorkshire Pullman' come immediately to mind.

Most steam-hauled titled trains carried coachboards and the majority of the locomotives sported headboards on the top or bottom lamp irons, making them easily identifiable from lineside. In this day and age, lamp irons are no longer a requirement for motive power, and apart from coach door route stickers or public address announcements, a titled train in the 1990s looks very much like its non-titled counterpart.

Anglia Region no longer has a 'Broadsman', a 'Fenman', a 'Hook Continental' or a 'Day Continental' from Liverpool Street but it has got a 'Britannia' and a 'Loreley', both of which emanate from Harwich Parkeston Quay; albeit only formed of Class 156 'Super Sprinters', but then one cannot have everything. The one locomotive-hauled named train currently operating from Liverpool Street is the 'East Anglian' to Norwich, a title dating back to 1937.

In addition to the 'Flying Scotsman', Eastern Region has always retained the 'Aberdonian', and in later years has reintroduced the 'Talisman', the 'Yorkshire Pullman' and the 'Tees-Tyne Pullman' names for some of their InterCity 125 services; the 'Yorkshire Pullman' now being Class 91-hauled, with the

Below:
Having run round its train, Class 37/4 No 37429 *Eisteddfod Genedlaethol* **departs from Shrewsbury on 30 June, with the 09.32 Pwllheli-Euston titled train, 'The Snowdonian'.**

other two services likely to follow suit upon completion of the East Coast electrification programme. A number of the more recently introduced named trains, such as the various 'Executives' to Hull and Bradford and the 'Highland Chieftain', take the place of much older titles, such as the 'Elizabethan', the 'Heart of Midlothian', the 'Queen of Scots', the 'White Rose' and the 'Northumbrian'.

Other new titles have been bestowed upon some 'Sprinter' services from Newcastle which rejoice in being the 'Borderer', the 'Galloway Enterprise', the Ayreshire Trader', the 'Tyne Trader' and the 'Tyne Enterprise'. Unless the conductor advises his 'customers' that they are travelling in a titled train, however, it is doubtful whether many of them would be aware of it — unless some entrepreneur has thought to have it printed on the paper cups used for drinks by the on-board trolley service!

The Midland line from Marylebone again has its 'Master Cutler', and also a new train, which started life as the 'Nottingham Pullman' but was later changed to the 'Robin Hood Pullman'; both are HSTs and both are likely to remain so for some time to come unless agreement is reached for electrification to Sheffield. Plying to and

Approaching Stafford, Class 90 No 90012 powers the 08.25 Glasgow Central-Poole InterCity service, 'The Wessex Scot'. Diesel traction, in the shape of an ILRA Pool Class 47/4 will take over the train at Birmingham New Street with arrival at Poole scheduled for 17.18.

from Euston, one can utilise a named sleeping car train and doze as the 'Night Aberdonian', 'Night Scotsman', 'Night Caledonian' or 'Royal Highlander' cross paths overnight, heading over the English/ Scottish border. Day travel can be taken in one of the newer titled trains, such as the Pullmans which carry the names of Lancashire, Manchester, Merseyside and Birmingham, the 'Welsh Dragon' (or 'Y Ddraig Gymreig' if you cannot understand English) or the Saturdays only 'Snowdonian' — or you can savour names of days gone by with the 'Irish Mail', the 'Cambrian Coast Express' (also Saturdays only), the 'Royal Highlander' and the 'Clansman', all these titles being still in use as well as the previously mentioned 'Royal Scot'. Early risers can take the 05.57 'John Peel' from Carlisle to Euston but, strangely, no such titled train appears in the timetable for a return journey.

Famous names which no longer appear in services to and from Euston include the 'Caledonian', the 'Comet', the 'Lakes Express', 'Lancastrian' and 'Manxman', together with the 'Merseyside Express', 'Midday Scot', 'Midlander', 'Palatine' and 'Red Rose'.

Although the Southern Region can no longer boast an 'Atlantic Coast Express', the Western Region can! A Saturdays Only HST from Paddington to Newquay now carries this title but, unlike the original, it no longer has nine portions for Bude, Exmouth, Ilfracombe, Okehampton, Padstow, Plymouth, Seaton, Sidmouth and Torrington! West Country InterCity services to and from Paddington still include the famed 'Cornish Riviera' and the well known 'Torbay Express' and 'Royal Duchy', but no longer a 'Bristolian', a 'Mayflower' or a 'Merchant Venturer'. To replace them, however, one can travel on

the 'Golden Hind Pullman' and the 'West Country Pullman', the 'Brunel' and the 'Armada'.

The 'South Wales Pullman' has not been seen in the timetables for a number of years but there is a new 'St David Pullman' in addition to the revamped 'Red Dragon Pullman', and in addition one can still visit the western extremities of Dyfed by way of the 'Pembroke Coast Express' and the newer 'Hibernian' to Fishguard Harbour. For the Cathedral Towns, the 'Cheltenham Spa' and 'Cathedrals Expresses' are still names currently in use, and like the much later 'Cotswold and Malvern Express', all are now formed of HSTs. Other than the prolific 'Network Expresses' on the 'Birmingham Direct' route, the only locomotive-hauled named train now operating within Western Region is the 'Night Riviera' to Penzance.

Once, the named trains of Southern Region were legion. Apart from the 'Atlantic Coast Express' already mentioned, prestige services from Waterloo, Victoria and Charing Cross used to include the 'Golden Arrow', the 'Night Ferry', the 'Bournemouth Belle', 'Brighton Belle', 'Devon Belle' and 'Kentish Belle', together with the 'Royal Wessex' and 'Man of Kent'. The 'Royal Wessex' has been resurrected in the guise of a Class 442 'Wessex Electric' unit and 'Bournemouth Belle' has operated as a Saturday special with all-Pullman stock. Just two of the many Class 421 electric services to Portsmouth carry the

new names (for trains at least) of 'Victory' and 'Mary Rose' but the names appear only on the Waterloo departure board, the trains themselves looking exactly the same as their un-named counterparts.

Inter-Regional services are today particularly well-endowed with titles, with those to and from Scotland the most prolific; the 'Devon Scot', 'Dorset Scot', 'Cornish Scot', 'Sussex Scot' and 'Wessex Scot' are all diagrammed for locomotive haulage, with the long-range fuel tank fleet of class 47/4s being the usual form of motive power. Names from the past which are still currently in use are the 'Cornishman', 'Devonian' and 'Northumbrian'.

Currently, more titled trains than ever before cross the England/Scotland border daily, but there are no longer any of the named Glasgow-Aberdeen expresses which once carried the celebrated epithets of 'Granite City', 'St Mungo', 'Grampian' and 'Bon-Accord' within the boundaries of Scottish Region. With present day services between Glasgow and Aberdeen being hourly, to name some of the trains would now really be superfluous. However, Scottish tradition should never be underestimated, and at some time in the future it would not be a great surprise if this colourful quartet was not returned from apparant oblivion.

Named trains operating within Scotland in 1990 are the 'Capital Enterprise' between Glasgow, Edinburgh and Stranraer, the 'Lord of the Isles' between Edinburgh and Mallaig/Oban, and the 'Orcadian' and 'Hebridean Heritage' from Inverness to Wick/Thurso and Kyle of Lochalsh, respectively; all Class 156 'Super Sprinters' — oh, and I nearly forgot the 'Lochaber', a new name for a new decade of steam-haulage between Fort William and Mallaig.

Above:
A titled train from steam days which had its name resurrected for a short time, but has now disappeared from the timetables again, was the 09.00 service from Poole to Newcastle, the 'Northumbrian', seen here at Aynho Junction, south of Banbury, on 3 March hauled by Class 47/4 No 47519.

Left:
Looking exactly the same as any other of the fast buffet services from Portsmouth Harbour to Waterloo, the 08.06 departure nevertheless bears a title of 'The Victory'. On 21 August, the train passes through Surbiton, on the last leg of the journey into London, formed of Class 421/5 4CIG No 1301 leading Class 412/3 4BIG No 2305.

Left:
Class 156 'Super Sprinter' No 156432 forming the 12.54 Newcastle-Stranraer train, 'The Galloway Express', speeds past Corby Gates and approaches Wetheral on 23 May. *Brian Beer*

Unusually, there are two weekday Class 442 'Wessex Electrics' each way to and from Waterloo, both bearing the name 'The Royal Wessex', one to and from Weymouth and the other to and from Poole. Both Weymouth services are early morning ones and both the Poole trains operate in the evenings. Approaching New Malden on 14 April, units Nos 2402/2409 form the 08.15 'Royal Wessex' for Weymouth.

The 17.03 Euston-Holyhead InterCity service carries its title both in Welsh and in English, 'Y Ddraig Gymreig/The Welsh Dragon', but so far as is known, none of the train's senior conductors has yet attempted to refer to the Welsh pronunciation over the public address system, at least not at the London end of the journey! On a sunny 28 April, the train hares through Cheddington headed by Class 86/2 No 86251 *The Birmingham Post*.

12
International Locomotives

Colin Boocock
All photographs by the author unless otherwise credited

The sight of a Netherlands Railways English Electric 350hp diesel shunting locomotive in a Dutch railway yard often excites the British railway enthusiast travelling abroad. Seeing a familiar machine perhaps makes him or her feel 'at home'. But what would excite a French railway enthusiast on a rail journey through Yugoslavia, or Portugal, for example? Could a Swedish railwayman see locomotives in Romania that make him feel 'at home'? Is it at all likely that a Norwegian or a Dane would recognise diesel locomotives in Hungary?

A fascinating study is in fact possible of all the classes of locomotive which appear simultaneously in the stock books of differ-ent Continental railways. This article only covers the present day, but the keen loco-motive student may back-track through his-tory to find that 'USA' 0-6-0Ts, Prussian 'P-8' 4-6-0s and Austrian 0-10-0s, for example, were all common sights on the railways of several different countries.

The 15 years during which six second-hand British Railways Class EM2 Co-Cos operated in Holland as part of the 1,500Vdc NS fleet ought not to qualify for inclusion in this article: the locomotives were not run-ning in the two countries simultaneously. I

Below:
An English Electric 350hp 0-6-0 diesel shunter based on the LMS design and used for the War Department, Netherlands Railways No 646 is seen stabled at Utrecht, Netherlands.

would, however never be forgiven by British readers for leaving them out!

Probably the most widely-spread diesel class to work in Western Europe has been the Nohab/General Motors Co-Co and A1A-A1A group of designs of 1,425 to 1,950hp dat-ing from the 1950s and early 1960s. The nearest of these to the UK were the green Belgian Classes 52, 53 and 54. Around 30 of these survive in rebuilt (and almost unrecog-nisable) form, and an unrebuilt locomotive of Class 54 is preserved. Neighbouring Lux-embourg has almost eliminated its Class 1600 red-liveried version of the same thing. But in Denmark there are many locomotives of almost identical outline still in service as Classes MX and MY, in the attractive red and black livery of DSB. Also, the Norwegians have a couple of dozen Co-Cos in their darker red. Swedish Railways, despite being

in the country of origin of the Nohab/GM locomotive family, were down to one example by 1989.

The greatest surprise for Nohab/GM followers is the presence of several examples of the same type in formerly- communist Hungary. They still operate out of Budapest Deli (South) station, are painted red all over and are immaculately turned out!

The Scandinavian influence extends into its exported electric locomotive designs, but in the cases described below, the locomotives are not necessarily manufactured in Sweden. Most Swedish Railways (SJ) express passenger trains are hauled by smart, orange Bo-Bo electrics of the 'Rc' series, which range from 'Rc1 to 'Rc6' The 'Rc2' was so successful as a light, compact locomotive making good use of solid state rectification equipment that the Austrian Federal Railways (OBB) purchased 10 as their Class 1043 to evaluate them over the Tauern line. They retained their Swedish orange livery, as do most of the large number of similar locomotives which run on the 25kV lines in Yugoslavia. The difference is that the Yugoslav locomotives are built in Yugoslavia by a number of manufacturers including Rade Koncar of Zagreb.

The odd place where this observer did not expect to see a Swedish designed locomotive was in Romania! However, as a result of a deal between Romanian Railways (CFR) and Yugoslav railways (JZ), Romania has been exchanging with Yugoslavia two new 7,000hp Co-Cos built in Craiova for three new

4,900hp Bo-Bos ('Rc' type) built in Zagreb. Both types use ASEA designed equipment. One feels that Romania gets the better bargain here! Why the author saw a JZ Swedish-style Bo-Bo in Belgrade painted in Romanian colours, one cannot tell. Perhaps one of the Yugoslav republics has adopted as standard the Romanian livery of two-tone grey, having received some Co-Cos in those colours.

Yugoslavia also features in the French connection, indeed in two ways. Travellers from France will already be bored with the single-cab Brissonneau et Lotz Bo-Bo diesel electrics, which start at 580hp and rarely rise above 810hp. Thus, a Frenchman seeing them at work on short freights and in yards in Zagreb and Belgrade is unlikely to match the excited response of a British gent seeing a clone of a Class 50 in Portugal, for example. Indeed the French holidaymaker journeying across the south of Portugal by train would be less than pleased to find his short train headed by a red version of the slow, under-powered Brissonneau et Lotz machines.

On the other hand, seeing a French-built Alsthom C-C *monomoteur* dc locomotive in

the smart livery of Slovenian Railways at Ljubliana is likely to inspire confidence in any railway enthusiast about to make a journey across the north of Yugoslavia! And the French again have not been slow in providing Portugal with powerful, C-C freight diesel electrics for the hilly routes in the south of that delightful country. Nor have they neglected to persuade the fastidious Dutch to buy Alsthom B-B electric locomotives for their principal intercity locomotive-hauled trains. All these types have their near equivalents on the SNCF in France.

Anyone who ventures further afield into Eastern Europe will have become familiar with another class of international locomotive. Known as Class l20 in East Germany, the Russian-built Co-Co diesel electrics of around 2,000hp, which date back to the 1960s and early 1970s, are also visible in large numbers in Poland, Czechoslovakia and Hungary. Some of the Hungarian ones belong to the international railway GySEV (Gyor-Sopron-Ebenfurti Vasut) which crosses over into Austria, so that Russian Co-Cos could be seen at Ebenfurt, at least before the GySEV line was recently electrified.

Other East European classes such as Skoda electric Bo-Bos (Czechoslovakia and Bulgaria), Romanian Sulzer Co-Co diesel electrics (Romania and Poland) and the standard Romanian Co-Co electrics also appear in a number of different countries.

This selection of international locomotives is far from exhaustive. The interested reader

Left:
Two newish Nohab/GM Co-Cos (now Class 52) head a mineral train through Namur station, Belgium, in 1961.

Below:
A pair of Nohab/GM Co-Cos rest at Trondheim, Norway, after arriving from Bødo with the overnight sleeping car train, one morning in 1973.

Bottom:
Seen on its home territory, Swedish Railways 'Rc2' Bo-Bo No 1086, waits to depart from Halsingborg with an international train for Oslo in 1980.

Above:
A Jugoslav-built example of the 'Rc2' design, No 441-753 stands in Belgrade terminus as a Russian-built EMU arrives alongside on 30 August 1990.

Right:
Swedish-designed, Jugoslav-built, working in Romania! CFR's 'Rc2'-type No 43-0096 stands at Gura Vaii on 6 September 1990. It is allocated to, and decorated at, the depot at Cerensebes. Note the front window curtains: the equipment compartment side windows have more of the same.

is encouraged to go abroad and look wider afield, to see for himself or herself a fascinating scene that is forever changing. For a first essay into this subject, why not go and discover a class of modern diesel locomotive which can be seen both in Denmark and Spain?

(Answers, please, on a postcard to the Editor).

Right:

Brissonneau et Lotz 625hp Bo-Bo diesel electric No 040 DE 132 stands at Gare du Nord, Paris, in 1959.

Right:

This class of B&L light Bo-Bo-diesel electric is widely seen in France, Portugal, Luxembourg and Jugoslavia. This Jugoslavian example, JS No 643.029, was built by Duro Dakovic of Slavonski Brod. It was photographed on 17 September 1987.

Right:

Motive power on Portugal's Algarve Coast line is almost exclusively B&L Bo-Bos of around 800hp. One is seen leaving Portimao with the 16.45 Lagos-Barriero on 6 August 1986.
Mary Boocock

SNCF dual voltage 25kV/1,500V B-B No 22267 sweeps through Menton on the French Mediterranean coast with a through train from Belgium in 1983.

Not a French backwater but the Portuguese main line from the Algarve coast to Lisbon. CC No 1904 pulls away from Messines with the up 'Sotavento' from Faro to Barriero on 9 August 1986.

13
Steam in East Germany Today

Andrew Fox
All photographs by the author

Amid the dramatic events in Eastern Europe during 1989, with the fall of the 'Iron Curtain', nowhere were the consequences more far-reaching than in the German Democratic Republic. There, a process was set in motion which led to a united currency and the end of border restrictions by July 1990, followed by the complete formal reunification of Germany in October 1990 and national German elections that December.

One of the last outposts of European steam during the 1980s, East Germany bade farewell to regular standard gauge steam in October 1988, although a varied fleet of preserved locomotives continued to see frequent use not only on special trains but also making occasional appearances on regular timetabled services.

The disappearance of steam on the standard gauge served only to emphasise the wealth of steam activity still to be seen on the *Deutsche Reichsbahn* (DR) narrow gauge lines. Although a gradual process of attrition had seen much of the once-extensive and numerous narrow gauge lines in East Germany closed during the 1960s and 1970s, relatively little was lost during the 1980s, with the exception of the wonderful Wolkenstein-Johstadt line. The DR entered the 1990s with eight separate systems on three different gauges, with the overwhelming majority of services still steam-hauled. Nothing comparable existed anywhere else in Europe, least of all in West Germany, where the Deutsche Bundesbahn had rid itself of such narrow gauge lines many years before. The narrow gauge lines of the Deutsche Reichsbahn owed their survival entirely to the political and economic system which dominated East Germany until 1989. This was one which gave a leading role to public transport, particularly the railways, for both goods and passenger traffic. Under the communist system, ownership of private cars was very limited by Western European standards, as was

the significance of freight haulage by road. This situation was in stark contrast to the proliferation of private cars and road hauliers which has since the 1950s become the accepted norm in the West. Above all, the primitive state of the road system in East Germany placed great limitations on what could feasibly be carried by this means. Especially in some of the more remote, rural areas, where the roads have barely been improved since the war, DR's lines continued to be the only practical means of freight transport.

With the narrow gauge steam locomotive fleet becoming increasingly difficult to maintain, and with hard-worked locomotives reaching the point where major rebuilds including reboiling, and even complete replacement, would become necessary, DR decided in the late 1980s on a programme which would almost entirely dieselise those

narrow gauge lines for which a continuing role was identified.

On the metre gauge Harz system, by far the longest of the surviving narrow gauge lines, the chosen method was to rebuild standard gauge Class 110 centre-cab Bo-Bo diesels by placing them on two 1,000mm gauge six-wheel bogies. The first of the rebuilds, Class 199[8] No 199 863, arrived at Wernigerode on 21 November 1988, followed during the following months by a further three, with a total of 30 examples on order.

For the 750mm gauge lines in Saxony, new diesels were to be supplied, built in Romania to a design developed from a series of locomotives built in Bulgaria. The plans envisaged construction of as many as 30 locomotives of 900hp, with the first to be delivered in the autumn of 1990.

Developments subsequent to the events of November 1989 had a dramatic effect on the

Right:
Saxon Meyer 0-4-4-0T No 99 1568 stands outside Mügeln shed after working the 07.35 Oschatz-Mügeln freight on Friday 14 September 1990. Built by Hartmann in 1910 as one of no fewer than 96 examples of Saxon State Railways Class IV K, No 99 1568 was one of 25 members of the class rebuilt with new boilers by the Deutsche Reichsbahn during the 1960s.

Right:

**Standard Class 99^{177x} 2-10-2T No 99 1789 storms
out of Seifersdorf past a fine plantation of
telegraph poles at 07.10 on Monday 17 September
1990 with the 06.28 Freital Hainsberg-Kurort
Kipsdorf. 24 members of this class were built for
the DR between 1952 and 1956 as a development
of the similar pre-war Class 99^{173x} in order to
renew the 750mm gauge locomotive fleet
following World War 2.**

future of the DR's narrow gauge operations.
By mid-1990 with the advent of a common
currency and the opening up of East Germany to trade with the West, it was clear that
much of East German industry was outdated,
inefficient and produced poor quality goods
for which there was little demand. It had sur-
vived in this form only due to the degree of
centralised state control which characterised
the old regime. During 1990 many busi-
nesses closed, while others went on to short-
time working as it became clear how great
the task of reconstructing the East German
economy would be. Unemployment — virtually unknown in the old German Democratic Republic — became an ever-worsening
problem.

At the same time some East Germans
began to realise that many of DR's minor
lines faced a very bleak future in the united
Germany, especially under a united German
Railways, with their equivalents in the Federal Republic having been closed perhaps 30
years before. The free-market system, with
much more money invested in road transport, would almost certainly regard such
lines as uneconomic and redundant. The
only realistic way to secure the future of at
least some of the narrow gauge lines would
be to promote them as tourist attractions,
since in their existing form as a common
carrier within the ordinary transport infrastructure their destiny was almost certain
run-down and closure as being no longer
necessary or financially viable once local
roads were improved.

The possibility of this new role for the
lines would also fit very well with the need to
develop any potential industry in East Germany which could help to support the ailing
economy and to create much-needed
employment. Under the old regime only a
very limited tourist industry had existed —
this in a country with some beautiful scenery
and historic towns, but relatively few specific
tourist attractions, and generally with very
poor roads. The narrow gauge lines would
therefore have the potential to help develop a
tourist industry and thereby at the same
time safeguard their own future, if only the
opportunity were grasped.

Keeping the lines as tourist attractions
would mean keeping steam, and this,
together with the threat which hung over
them in their traditional role, meant a reap-
praisal of the dieselisation plans. The order
for diesels for the metre gauge Harz system
was cut back from 30 to 10 locomotives.
These lines had considerable tourist potential due to their location, but would still
require diesels for any remaining freight
operations and as a reserve for the steam
fleet. Meanwhile by the end of 1990 it was

clear that the proposed 750mm gauge diesels
from Romania had been cancelled, and that
any dieselisation of these lines would be
much less extensive than had previously
been envisaged. Realistically, there might
still be a need for some diesel locomotives on
any of the lines to be retained, if only as a
back-up to steam. With the possible closure
of some lines and the newly recognised
importance of steam power on those to stay
open, the programme of mass dieselisation
was no longer relevant.

With the new value placed on the retention of steam power as an attraction in its
own right, the DR was still faced with the
growing maintenance problems posed by its
existing fleet. It therefore approached the
Swiss Locomotive Works, SLM of Win-
terthur, with a view to obtaining a series of
brand new locomotives and possibly reboiler-
ing the more modern examples of the DR
narrow gauge fleet.

One of the most remarkable developments
concerned the 750mm gauge system based
on the town of Zittau in the far southeast of
the country. This had been due to close in
May 1990 to make way for a large open-cast
mining project. Fortunately, however, this

Above:

**The sight of a Saxon Meyer on regular passenger
services returned to East Germany during the
summer of 1990, when No 99 1608, normally kept
in reserve, was pressed into duty on the Cranzahl
– Oberwiesenthal line due to an extreme motive
power shortage. On Tuesday 18 September 1990 it
leaves Neudorf with the 17.33 from Cranzahl.
No 99 1608 was built in 1921 as Saxon State
Railways No 198, the last of 96 members of Class
IV K, first built in 1892**

project was abandoned due to the move away
from burning the soft brown coal mined in
East Germany, a very poor source of energy
in terms of calorific value and a very serious
cause of pollution, which has been recognised as a major problem in East Germany as
well as other East European countries. Due
to the planned closure of the Zittau system,
maintenance over the last couple of years
had been kept to an absolute minimum, with
the result that by 1990 the track was in a
very poor condition, and featured many
speed restrictions. As a result of the decision
to keep the line open, it was necessary to
make up for the major backlog of maintenance. For this reason the system was com-

Table 1 January 1991
Surviving DR steam lines

(i) Harzquerbahn/Selketalbahn
Gauge: 1,000mm
Total Length: 118.0km
Services: Passenger & Freight
Classes: †99^{59xx}, 99^{60xx}, 99^{61xx}, 99^{722x}, 99^{723x}, *$19900x$, *199^{01x}, *199^{3xx}, 199^{8xx}

(ii) Bad Doberan-Kühlungsborn
Gauge: 900mm
Total Length: 15.4km
Services: Passenger only
Classes: 99^{232x}, 99^{233x}

(iii) Putbus-Göhren
Gauge: 750mm
Total Length: 24.2km
Services: Passenger only
Classes: 99^{177x}, 99^{463x}, 99^{48xx}, *100^{9xx}

(iv) Radebeul-Radeburg
Gauge: 750mm
Total Length: 16.6km
Services: Passenger & Freight
Classes: 99^{177x}, †99^{15xx}, †99^{171x}

(v) Freital Hainsberg-Kurort Kipsdorf
Gauge: 750mm
Total Length: 26.3km
Services: Passenger & Freight
Classes: 99^{15xx}, 99^{173x}, 99^{177x}

(vi) Zittau-Jonsdorf/Oybin
Gauge: 750mm
Total Length: 16.1km
Services: Passenger & Freight
Classes: 99^{173x}, 99^{177x}, 99^{453x}

(vii) Cranzahl-Oberwiesenthal
Gauge: 750mm
Total Length: 17.4km
Services: Passenger & Freight
Classes: 99^{15xx}, 99^{173x}, 99^{177x}

(viii) Oschatz-Mügeln-Kemmlitz
Gauge: 750mm
Total Length: 17.3km
Services: Freight only
Class: 99^{15xx}

Notes:
* shunting and works trains only
† special trains only, not used in normal service

The narrow gauge lines of the Deutsche Reichsbahn as at January 1991.

Table 2
Steam Locomotives

Class	No Series	Wheel Arr	Built	Builder	Gauge	Total	Lines
99^{15xx}	99 1542-1608	0-4-4-OT	1899-1921	Hartmann	750mm	14	(iv) (v) (vii) (viii)
99^{171x}	99 1713	0-10-OT	1927	Hartmann	750mm	1	(iv)
99^{173x}	99 1731-1762	2-10-2T	1928-1933	Hartmann, Schwartzkof	750mm	14	(v) (vi) (vii)
99^{177x}	99 1771-1794	2-10-2T	1952-1956	Babelsberg	750mm	22	(iii) (iv) (v) (vi) (vii)
99^{232x}	99 2321-2323	2-8-2T	1932	Orenstein & Koppel	900mm	3	(vi)
99^{233x}	99 2331-2332	0-8-OT	1951	Babelsberg	900mm	2	(ii)
99^{453x}	99 4532	0-8-OT	1924	Orenstein & Kopel	750mm	1	(vi)
99^{463x}	99 4632-4633	0-8-OWT	1914-1925	Vulcan	750mm	2	(iii)
99^{48xx}	99 4801-4802	2-8-OT	1938	Henschel	750mm	2	(iii)
99^{59xx}	99 5901-5903	0-4-4-OT	1897	Jung	1,000mm	3	(i)
99^{59xx}	99 5906	0-4-4-OT	1918	Karlsruhe	1,000mm	1	(i)
99^{60xx}	99 6001	2-6-2T	1939	Krupp	1,000mm	1	(i)
99^{61xx}	99 6101-6102	0-6-OT	1914	Henschel	1,000mm	2	(i)
99^{722x}	99 7222	2-10-2T	1931	Schwartskopf	1,000mm	1	(i)
99^{723x}	99 7231-7247	2-10-2T	1954-1956	Babelsberg	1,000mm	17	(i)

Diesel Locomotives

Class	No Series	Wheel Arr	Built	Builder	Gauge	Total	Lines
100^{9xx}*	100 901	0-6-ODH	1944	Gmeinder	750mm	1	(iii)
199^{00x}*	199 005-006	0-6-ODM	1964	Babelsberg	1,000mm	2	(i)
199^{01X}*	199 010	0-6-ODH	1984†	DR	1,000mm	1	(i)
199^{3xx}*	199 301	0-6-ODH	1966	Babelsberg	1,000mm	1	(i)
199^{8xx}	199 861-872	C-C DH	1988#	DR Stendal	1,000mm	4	(i)

Notes:
* shunting and works trains only
† rebuilt from standard gauge Class Kö II
# rebuilt from standard gauge Class 110

January 1991

Right:

Class 99⁵⁹ˣˣ Mallet 0-4-4-0T No 99 5902, built by Jung in 1897, stands at Wernigerode Westerntor with an excursion to Benneckenstein on Sunday 23 September 1990. This locomotive was overhauled and returned to service in May 1990 for use on special trains with a rake of vintage carriages. The last use of Class 99⁵⁹ˣˣ on regular service trains ended in the late 1980s on the Selketalbahn section of the Harz system. 12 of these compound Mallets were built for the newly-opened Nordhausen-Wernigerode line between 1897 and 1901, and proved highly succesful.

Below:

By the 1980s the freight-only Oschatz-Mügeln-Kemmlitz line was all that remained of a once extensive 750mm gauge system. In latter years it was operated exclusively by veteran Class 99¹⁵ˣˣ O-4-4-0T Saxon Meyers. No 99 1561 leaves Mugeln on Wednesday 19 September 1990, heading for the kaolin works at Kemmlitz, by this time the main source of traffic for the line.

pletely closed for a period of no less than 11 weeks from 17 September 1990 in order to carry out the complete renewal of the permanent way.

The strong impression existed in late 1990 that many East Germans, particularly at a local level, were doing what they could to safeguard the future of the narrow gauge lines while these were still operated by a separate DR management. A programme of renewal and modernisation for the narrow gauge lines would present the future united German Railways with a *fait accompli,* making it difficult to close lines which had recently received major investment. Alternatively, such a programme of improvements might enable the privatisation of at least some of the lines as viable going concerns. A positive effort to secure the survival of the lines was shown by the introduction of improved timetables on several of them in late 1990 and early 1991, with accelerated and more regular passenger services.

However, the success of promoting DR's narrow gauge lines as tourist carriers appears central to their long-term future. In this respect the country was in a unique position as it entered the 1990s, having lines which were basically in good working order, with complete motive power and rolling stock fleets as well as a dedicated workforce. Moreover most of the remaining lines were situated in attractive areas of the country,

already developing as holiday and spa centres — the Harz mountains, Saxony and the Baltic coast. Indeed the Cranzahl-Oberwiesenthal line is a prime means of access to a major ski resort, while the Radebeul-Radeburg and Freital Hainsberg-Kurort Kipsdorf lines are already popular for excursions by the inhabitants of Dresden. The one line which is relatively unfavourably located is the freight-only Oschatz-Mügeln-Kemmlitz line, which faces the most precarious future.

Many fine minor and narrow gauge railways were thoughtlessly closed during the 1950s and 1960s across Western Europe, with little regard for their potential, only in some cases for enthusiasts subsequently to expend considerable money and effort in order to re-open them, and in other cases leaving rural areas deprived for ever of a valuable part of the local infrastructure. It is

to be hoped that the East Germans do not allow such a mistake to be made in the 1990s, and that the wonderful narrow gauge railway heritage is adapted and promoted, to be used and enjoyed by generations to come.

The first privatisation to be announced concerned the metre gauge Harz system, consisting of the former Nordhausen-Wernigeroder Eisenbahn and the Gernrode-Harzgeroder Eisenbahn. These were not absorbed into the DR until 1949, and now 42 years later they were to be 'de-nationalised', their operation being taken over by a group of local councils. Plans for developing the lines included re-opening the branch line from Schierke to the summit of the Brocken — the highest mountain in the Harz range, and a popular tourist attraction. Due to its proximity to the former inter-German border, regular passenger services on this line were suspended in 1961, with the remaining military traffic ceasing in 1980. The cost of rehabilitating the Brocken line was estimated at approximately DM3 million. Further proposals included investing DM40 million to provide radio signalling, a fleet of 12 two-car diesel railcars and a snow blower. The railcars would take over regular passenger duties for the whole system. This, together with the disappearance of freight operations would see the end of steam on all but special excursion/enthusiast services; a sad but perhaps inevitable development.

14
Traction 2000

Roger Ford
Technical Editor of Modern Railways

Over the past decade, rail traction technology in Britain advanced at a faster rate than at any time in railway history. At the heart of this development were the microprocessor and power electronics. Today, we can see the first results of this revolution in revenue earning service. However, the full benefits will start to become apparent over the next decade, as a wide range of new traction, now on order or planned, starts to enter service.

Mighty micro
Microprocessor controlled traction equipments are not new. What has forced the pace of change has been the combination of growing power and computing speed with plummeting cost. As a result, railway engineers have been able to base a whole new generation of equipment on advanced microprocessor systems, able to control an unprecedented range of functions.

Super switches
On its own, a micro is like a brain without a body. It can think, but it has no muscle. To control power it needs to be able to switch electric current on and off.

A thyristor is simply an electronic switch. Small electrical signals from a micro can control thousands of volts and amps. However, in its original form, the thyristor has one big disadvantage. You can switch it on — 'gate it' in engineering parlance. But the only way to turn it off is to reverse the voltage across it. This required complex and highly expensive circuits to produce three phase drives with alternating current motors. Then, engineers made the vital breakthrough. They developed a thyristor which could be gated 'on' and 'off'. This is the 'gate turn off' thyristor, or gto.

Combine the microprocessor's control with the gto's electrical muscle and the traction engineer can provide pretty well any combination of power and performance that the railway business needs — at an affordable price. These technologies will be the basis of the new locomotives and trains entering service on BR in the coming decade.

Ultimate DC locomotive
But before we get on to the three phase drive revolution, mention must be made of the ultimate example of direct current drive, probably in the world.

When the Class 91 went out to tender in 1985, the gto revolution had only just begun. But British engineers had raised the direct current traction motor to a fine art. Thus, the Class 91 combines state-of-the-art microprocessor control with direct current motors 30% more powerful than those in the Class 87. The result is a locomotive unmatched for cost-effective high performance. For example, at today's prices a Class 91 would cost around £1.75 million. In contrast, a similarly rated power car for the German IC-E high speed train costs nearly £3 million.

Given the outstanding reliability of the Class 91, plus the fact that its bogies and suspension could handle much higher speeds than its nominal 140mph maximum, more could well be ordered, to upgrade the West Coast main line.

Energy saver
However, three phase drive is set to dominate the new traction scene on BR from now on. In the autumn of 1991, the first Class 465 Networker electric multiple units are due to be delivered to Network SouthEast's Kent and southeast London services. These trains would not exist had not the gto thyristor made three-phase drive commercially viable.

Following the boom in commuter traffic in the 1980s, Network SouthEast faced the prospect of increasingly severe overcrowding unless it could provide extra capacity — quickly. With track and station capacity fixed, the only way to provide more seats was to run longer trains, faster.

Unfortunately, with existing technology, longer, faster trains would use more energy.

Below:
**Currently the last word in electric traction, the Class 91 is doomed to get left behind by progress as technology moves in new directions. However, this highly efficient design contains a number of features that will influence future thinking.
No 91009 is seen at speed on a King's Cross-Leeds train between Helpston and Tallington in April 1990.** *J. H. Cooper-Smith*

This would not only increase the operating costs but would require substantial upgrading of the electrical power supplies. These costs meant that investment in extra capacity could not be justified. Fortunately, the arrival of affordable three-phase drive completely changed the cost equation. For a start, three-phase drive provides particularly effective regenerative braking. This is where the traction motors are run as generators to slow the train. The electricity they produce is returned to the power supply for use by other trains.

Regenerative braking shows 24% energy saving. It also cuts brake pad replacement costs, the largest single item of train maintenance expenditure on Network SouthEast.

At the same time alternating current motors are smaller and lighter than the direct current equivalent, allowing more power to be packed into a train. As a result, the Class 465 will give a 10% reduction in journey times, effectively increasing line capacity.

Networker family
Class 465 is the first of what will be a family of Networker electric multiple units. Financial pressures have slowed the planned building schedule in the short term, but by the year 2000 it will be Networkers everywhere on Network SouthEast.

For operation with 25kV alternating current power supplies north of the Thames, there will be the Class 341. The first batch of these trains, for London, Tilbury and Southend services, will follow the Class 465 fleet through the workshops. With ac electrification, regenerative braking is even more effective. Energy savings of 30% have already been achieved in trials with the Class 316 prototype on the Colchester branch.

Next will come the fleet of Class 471 outer-suburban trains for Kent Coast services, with deliveries starting in 1995/96. Then it will be back north of the Thames for a second batch of Class 341 Networkers to run through the

CrossRail tunnel linking Paddington and Liverpool Street stations. CrossRail should open in 1998/99.

If British Rail builds its high speed link between London and the Channel Tunnel, the first 125mph Networker, the Class 473, could be under construction by AD 2000.

Locomotives
For domestic passenger and freight services, British Rail is reasonably well-stocked with locomotives.

By AD 2000, services on the West Coast main line should have been accelerated with the introduction of InterCity 250. Whether trains really will run regularly at 155mph on this busy route remains to be seen. InterCity has proposed a new Class 93 three-phase drive 7,000hp electric locomotive for this duty. To meet the performance requirements, it might be necessary to have six powered axles. In this case we could see a Bo-Bo locomotive powering traction motors on the leading bogie of the following passenger vehicle. This was adopted for the first TGV and for the TransManche Super Trains.

However, I would put my money on an improved Class 91 for this duty. It should be remembered that the Class 91 was designed originally to replace APT, hauling tilting trains on the WCML. Its outstanding performance and reliability to date, plus an attractive price, could lead to a fleet of 91/1s in service some time after 1995.

IC125 replacement
A more intriguing question is posed by the Great Western main line. By 2000, the oldest IC125s will be approaching their 25th anniversary — a long time in front-line service.

Ideally, the electrification of Paddington for the Heathrow Express will extend in stages to, at least, Bristol and Cardiff. In that case a Class 93 could be justified for service on this, the first main line aligned for high speed.

But supposing that diesel traction has to remain in front line service on the GWML. Then, a considerable technical challenge would emerge. In terms of performance, the present IC125 power car has only a little more to offer. Certainly, the Valenta diesel engine could now be safely uprated to the 2,500hp planned when trains were purchased. While this would give a combined rating of 5,000hp, it must be remembered that one engine of an IC125 has to provide around 450hp for air conditioning and other services. If journey times on the GWML are to keep up with electrified services on the other InterCity routes, its diesel trains will need 6,000hp for traction. Ideally, the potential line speed should also be raised to 140mph.

One way of achieving this would be a new power car based on the Class 91 running gear. The critical factor is the choice of diesel engine.

British Rail's high speed trains are the toughest diesel application in the world. Only the Paxman Valenta has proved capable of standing up to the duty. A 16-cylinder Valenta, compared with the 12-cylinder in IC125, would give 3,300hp. Of the new generation of engines, the 12-cylinder Ruston will be available, rated at 3,000hp, from 1992.

For enthusiasts of high speed, high power, diesel traction, an unelectrified GWML offers the greatest chance of excitement at the turn of the century. Remember, that what is needed is the equivalent of a Class 55 Deltic output from an 80 tonnes-at-most Bo-Bo power car.

Freight diesels
With Railfreight traction, the crystal ball clouds a little. For Train Load Freight, the Class 60 diesel will form the basis for the heavy haul of coal, steel, oil and the other basic products.

There has been talk of a 75mph Class 60 for Railfreight Distribution duties and for Trainload services where journey time is more important than squeezing the maximum economy of scale out of the heaviest trains. This new locomotive was numbered Class 61 but went on to the back burner when doubts emerged over Railfreight Distribution's losses. It might be revived by Trainload Freight as the Class 62.

If Channel Tunnel Railfreight takes off as expected, something like the Class 61 could re-emerge for the non-electrified routes handling international traffic.

Also proposed is a mini-Class 60 for the coal business. This was designated Class 41 and recognises the fact that not all collieries can generate Class 60-sized loads. At 2,200-

Left:
Class 60 is very much state of the art in diesel technology, far more so than the much-hyped Class 59 American imports which attract the adulation of certain enthusiasts. No 60004, the first member of the class to carry Coal Sub-Sector livery, is seen at Thornaby during a Driver Training visit in October 1990. *Norman Barrington*

The Networker Turbos will represent something of a new departure in DMU technology, thanks to the determination of NSE to get what it wants, within tight constraints. The first bodyshell of a Class 165 coach to be completed and painted for demonstration purposes is seen here at BREL York in August 1990. *BREL*

2,800hp, it might be termed the modern equivalent of a Class 37. On its own it could handle maximum train loads from a number of collieries. Multiple operation would allow heavier loads to be hauled.

Electric freight

Since nationalisation, Railfreight has tended to share 'mixed traffic' designs with InterCity when it comes to electric locomotives. The last of these designs was the Class 90.

With the need for a locomotive to haul freight over the Southern Region and through the Channel Tunnel as far as the French terminal, Railfreight was able to purchase its first all-freight electric locomotive. This is the Class 92, which will also be BR's first three-phase drive locomotive.

Structurally, the Class 92 is derived from the Class 60. It also has a similar starting tractive effort, although the continuous rating is 6,700hp, more than double the Class 60's output. Three phase drive simplifies the provision of the dual voltage capability needed for operation on the Southern Region's 750V dc third rail supply and the 25kV ac overhead supply elsewhere in Britain and in the tunnel. In fact, the most demanding duty the Class 92 will face will not be in the Tunnel, but hauling 1,600 tonne trains over Shap and Beattock.

At present, BR has only 20 on order, but there are options for another 40. If freight through the Tunnel takes off and there is more electrification, Class 92s will be a familiar sight throughout the system by 2000. Some may be fitted with electric train heating, to haul international sleeping car trains through the Tunnel.

Golden oldies

By the end of the century, surviving Modernisation Plan diesels will be approaching their 40th birthday. How many, and what Classes, will survive depends on whether the financial case can be made for replacements.

For InterCity, a Class 47 replacement is urgently needed to improve reliability and reduce operating costs on cross country services. However, only a small quantity is required because of the availability of IC125 sets displaced by the East Coast main line electrification. If the replacement, designated Class 48, goes ahead, it will be around 2,500hp and perhaps have a Bo-Bo wheel arrangement.

The display mock-up of the nose end of a Networker EMU shows that these units will look as dramatically different from the 4EPBs they will replace as will their performance differ.
Peter McCormack

Above:
By AD2000 the '9ls' will be 'old hat' and Pacers will be decidedly long in the tooth but scenes such as this will probably still be commonplace. No 91004 stands at Leeds with Pacer No 142068 alongside.
Colin Boocock

Right:
Push-pull technology is here to stay. Met-Camm DVT225 No 82200 is seen undergoing tests for clearance and flexibility at the Railway Technical Centre, Derby. Les Nixon

As Class 60 deliveries build up, double heading of the heaviest freight trains by Class 47s and Class 37s will diminish. This should free a number of locomotives for scrapping or allocation to other duties. Build up of the Class 158 DMU fleet is having a similar effect on locomotives at present used on Regional passenger trains.

However, the new Sector liveries have highlighted the large number of departmental locomotives needed to maintain the railway. It is most unlikely that a financial case could be made to replace these locomotives with new equipment. Thus, the familiar Sulzer bark and English Electric whistle should still be heard in 2000 from the yellow and grey liveried fleet.

City movers
With no more Regional DMUs likely to be ordered, the focus has turned to the Passenger Transport Executives. Here, too, the three-phase drive revolution has begun in the form of the Class 323. Already on order for Birmingham, with options on further trains for Leeds, the high-performance, aluminium-bodied Class 323 shows the way forward, as BR seeks to improve commuter services in the great conurbations.

International
Finally, by 2000, high-speed international

trains will have become a familiar sight on at least the East and West Coast main lines. Now on order are the mighty Trans Manche Super Trains, Class 373 to BR.

With 18 coaches, plus two power cars with a combined rating of 16,000hp, the TMSTs will be the longest and most powerful trains ever seen on Britain's rails. Sadly, the limitations of the Network SouthEast dc power supply will hold them back to 90mph south of the Thames until the new high speed link is built.

However, when the East Coast main line is fitted with cab signalling we could see Class 373s and Class 91s running at 140mph on the East Coast main line. For the modern traction enthusiast, the 1990s are going to be a very exciting decade indeed.

15
Five of the Best

Robin Russell
All photographs by the author

After an upbringing in England when steam traction predominated, it was a fascinating experience to return in April 1990 and travel on some of the locomotive classes which I recall from my younger days.

I was able to compare British locomotive operation with practice on New Zealand's railways, as observed from the footplates of many preserved engines. These include a firing trip between Kingston and Lumsden on a 'Kingston Flyer' 4-6-2, Class 'Ab' and a short spell with the shovel on Phil Goldman's famous 'Ja' 4-8-2 No 1250 *Diana* on the NZ Railways (NZR) main line. Duties as a member of the footplate staff of the Glenbrook Vintage Railway, one of New Zealand's leading preservation operations, provided an additional perspective.

Following these experiences, five UK railways very generously provided me with cab passes; I proceeded to the lines concerned, armed with camera and notebook.

I started off in the 'Strong Country', a title which used to appear on lineside hoardings installed by a Hampshire brewery, depicting a Southern express at speed; steam-hauled, of course. On Easter Monday I arrived at Alton, eastern terminus of the 'Watercress Line'. Through the good offices of Ms M. Parker (PA to the Managing Director) and Locomotive Superintendent John Bunch, I was to ride on what is perhaps Britain's most exciting class of engine: an SR Bulleid Pacific in its original form.

I travelled in the train behind No 34105 *Swanage* on the 10-mile trip to Alresford, at the western end of the line, where I transferred to the engine. On board I was greeted by Driver J. Rooney, Fireman J. Gibbons and Trainee C. Egie. I immediately noticed the large coal, standard for the UK as I was to discover, but about twice the size of good quality NZ fuel as currently supplied. (NZR steam crews used to get ungraded coal, even on the main lines). Further, the fire was made up to a greater depth than I was accustomed to. The excellent Bulleid cab layout is well known, and compares favourably with the latest NZR steam locomotives; these, in common with most 'West Country' engines as built, are not fitted with ashpan dampers, but No 34105 is one of the few so equipped.

Our six-carriage train was soon on its way to Ropley, site of the locomotive depot and works. This portion of the trip was taken under easy steam, but even then I could hear the familiar rasp of the exhaust. On leaving Ropley, the engine was immediately opened out and the result was impressive. The steam-chest pressure gauge (an instrument

Above:
Mid Hants; No 34105 *Swanage* leaves Ropley for Alton, passing the MPD on the left.

not fitted to NZR locomotives) was soon round to 220 psi, cut-off was 40%; no sand was applied but we stormed up the 1 in 60/80 to the summit at Medstead & Four Marks without a trace of a slip. Although Bulleid Pacifics are not universally popular, in the right hands they are unbeatable. I recalled a trip on No 34092 *City of Wells* on the K&WVR, when 50% cut off and full regulator did not cause slipping, recounted in the 1982 *Railway World Annual*).

Once over the top at Medstead, the remainder of the journey was uneventful, although I was able to try my hand at a short spell of firing. The larger coal was harder to scoop up and a shovelful seemed to be heavier, but I managed to make it all go in the required position.

Below:
Mid Hants; Driver J. Rooney at the regulator of *Swanage*.

I left the Mid-Hants recalling the remarkable power and the evocative exhaust note of *Swanage* and also thinking about what has been achieved by the railway since it reopened the route 'Over the Alps'. The use of the Alton extension is now taken for granted, as is the restoration of so many fine locomotives. Looking ahead, the thought of four Bulleid Pacifics working on one railway is an exciting one which will almost certainly be realised in due course.

Whereas the Mid-Hants was a relief route for diverted expresses, my visit the following day was to a first-class main line, built to generous loading gauge and axle weight standards: the Great Central.

Upon arrival at Loughborough (where my first 12 years were spent) I proceeded to inspect the remains of the bridge which carried the double-track LNER line from Marylebone to Manchester over the four tracks of its LMS rival from St Pancras. When I was a schoolboy, the spotting fraternity often congregated near this bridge, in order to observe trains on both routes. (In the 1948 locomotive exchanges, all mixed-traffic classes passed over — and most passed under — it. One engine concerned was GWR 4-6-0 No 6990 *Witherslack Hall,* which is currently at Loughborough.) With the bridge now demolished, freight trains on the ex-LNER line north of this point take a spur facing towards Leicester at a new junction with the LMR route. Rebuilding of the bridge is a vital part of the plan to extend the Great Central Railway to Ruddington (south of Nottingham).

Leaving my thoughts of both past and future, I headed for the Great Central station (the displayed 1898 building date reveals how comparatively recently the GC main line was opened). I was introduced to Locomotive Chief Alan Grice, who issued the footplate pass arranged by Operations Manager Harold Porter. The engine for the day, working the one-engine-in-steam midweek service, was on loan from Tyseley: GWR 0-6-0PT No 7760. (We used to call them 'matchbox tanks', because of their shape — not their size.) The engine had only recently arrived at Loughborough, but it presented no problems to Driver W. Gwilt (who used to work Stanier Pacifics out of Euston) and Fireman B. Horsley.

Upon receiving the 'Right Away', we headed through the outskirts of Loughborough, climbing a gradient of predominantly 1 in 176 en route to Quorn. The station here is another in the classic Great Central style, of a road overbridge serving an island platform. We continued to climb at 1 in 264/330, past the scenic Swithland reservoir, to Rothley, southernmost terminus at the time of my visit. The engine had steamed freely,

again on large lumps of good quality coal. Driver Gwilt used a fairly small regulator opening: cut-off was hard to determine on the lever reverser. (This type of reverser was used on many NZR engines; more recent designs had compressed-air reversers, operated from the Westinghouse Air Brake supply. No use was made of the handwheels so common in Britain.) After running round the train at Rothley, the engine was recoupled and we returned to Loughborough.

The section of the railway south from Rothley to Leicester North (Birstall) is now open, extending the route mileage from 5 miles to 8½. Doubling of the track is planned, with a further idea for loops to create a total of four lines. The latter-day Great Central has achieved much (notably the restoration of No 71000 *Duke of Gloucester*), and is clearly not content to rest upon its laurels.

After my day in the open — and relatively flat — Leicestershire countryside, the Keighley & Worth Valley Railway was very different. Curves and gradients abound, hills rise on all sides. Another contrast is the green pastures juxtaposed with the chimneys of the 'dark satanic mills'. A similarity with the Loughborough trip was the use of a right-hand drive 0-6-0T for the midweek service. The engine in use on Wednesday 18 April was LMR 'Jinty' No 47279. (The 'Pannier' and 'Jinty' have wheel diameters of 4ft 7½in and 4ft 7in respectively. Remarkably, the almost identical figure of 4ft 6in was the standard driving-wheel diameter for the biggest and fastest NZR designs).

I observed No 47279 being prepared at the Haworth depot, the Responsible Officer for the day, I. Holt, having provided the footplate pass arranged by Traffic Manager Bill Black. I introduced myself to the engine crew: Driver R. Ingham (who was firing for the day), Fireman T. Reeve (who was driving) and Trainee Ms L. Walden who kindly travelled on the train while I had my ride.

This started on the second northbound (downhill) service of the day. After the run down to Keighley, the 'Jinty' was recoupled for the more interesting uphill journey. The engine was worked far harder than the 'Pannier', but was — again — master of its work. Immediately after leaving the terminus, trains encounter steep gradients on a sharp curve. After passing the site of the junction of the old GNR line to Queensbury, the line rises at 1 in 114/159 to Ingrow. Here is located the carriage museum, and the new home of the Bahamas Locomotive Society (which received a great welcome after its eviction from Dinting). Ingrow Tunnel (1 in 85) is followed by 1 in 56/64/60/90 past Damems (Britain's smallest station) and Oakworth, and through Mytholmes tunnel. After the Haworth stop, it is largely 1 in 68 to the end of the line at Oxenhope, to conclude just under five miles of exciting steam travel.

The KWVR — always looking ahead — is about to increase its support still further, by organising a children's club. Past achievements include the 1970 filming of *The Railway Children* and inaugurating the now widespread 'Santa Specials'; awards include 'Best Kept Station' and 'Independent Railway

of the Year'. One could — in lighter vein — add their achievement in devising the term 'festoon' to describe a railway photographer!

My visit the following day was to another Yorkshire line, the North Yorkshire Moors. Upon arrival, I received my pass from General Manager Frank Pearce and climbed on to the footplate of Southern 4-6-0 No 841, one of the final batch of 'S15' mixed traffic engines; this used to be painted green and named *Greene King*. It is now black and has no name — very authentic. The engine was already on the six-carriage train, tender first. As Driver M. Oliver, Fireman R. Stewart and Trainee G. Beautyman made room for me shortly before departure, I gave a thought to the effect of track gauge upon loading gauge: not as much as one might think. NZR operates on 3ft 6in gauge track, yet the cab of a 'Ja' 4-8-2 is as wide as one of the first series of Bulleid's lightweight Pacifics. Meanwhile, our 4-6-0's 18-mile trip began with gradients of 1 in 332/238 as far as Levisham. Here we crossed the impressive 'Austerity' 2-10-0 No 3672 *Dame Vera Lynn* heading a southbound train.

As we moved off again, the regulator was opened fully and cut-off set at 40% to cope

with gradients of 1 in 104/75/60/49. Ample steam was available, the fuel being made up to slightly above the fire door; quite the deepest fire I have observed. The climb then eased and was followed by level track across Fen Bog, the highest point on the line. As the train descended towards Grosmont, we could see the radar domes ('golf balls') of the Fylingdales early warning system on the eastern sky-line.

Just before Grosmont Tunnel is the motive power depot, currently being enlarged as a memorial to the late John Bellwood, CME, of the National Railway Museum at York. Driver Oliver obliged by stopping for me to catch a brief glimpse of SR 'Schools' 4-4-0 No 926 *Repton*, the first engine I ever fired (on the Cape Breton Steam Railway in Nova Scotia, Canada). I left the shed and walked through the foot tunnel to Grosmont, where the platform was being lengthened.

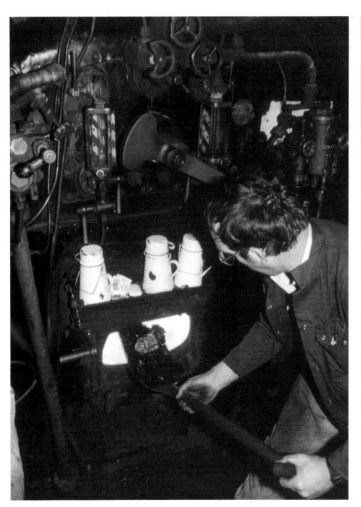

My return trip was on BR Standard 4MT 2-6-4T No 80135, so convenient to work that crews refer to it as 'the office'. Driver T. Newman, who welcomed me on board to meet Fireman P. Davis, had recently travelled to the West Highland line as support crew for LNER 'K1' 2-6-0 No 2005. Once out of Grosmont and through the tunnel, the main feature of the southbound journey is the 3-mile-plus climb at 1 in 49 to Goathland. The six carriages were hauled using 50% cut-off and full regulator; again, a very deep fire produced plenty of steam. The gradient subsequently eased to 1 in 90/100 up to Fen Bog.

All too soon the trip was over, and I was leaving Britain's second longest preserved line, highly scenic, with a remarkable stock of locomotives which includes the two named LMS 'Black Fives' and ER 'J72' 0-6-0T No 69023 *Joem* which had a spell as sole motive power on the East Somerset Railway.

The final event in my remarkable week of steam trains was a journey on the Bluebell Line, the first standard gauge preserved route and still a leader. On Sunday 22 April I arrived at Sheffield Park and was shown round the locomotive works and depot by Bulleid expert Roger Cruse; exhibits included

Right:
Bluebell; Driver John White at the controls of 'Q' No 541.

Below:
Bluebell; 'Q' No 541 approaches the Horsted Keynes outer home signal.

No 21C123 *Blackmore Vale* — an original 'West Country' which was probably restored to an even higher standard than *City of Wells*. Still being worked on was a modified example, No 34059 *Sir Archibald Sinclair*. Even further from completion was the Ivatt boiler destined to become part of a 'Brighton Atlantic'; this project has its critics, but I would like to see one of my favourite classes in action again. Express engines at present in service include 'Merchant Navy' No 35027 *Port Line* and 'Schools' No 928 *Stowe*.

From the locomotive area to the station, and I noted the splendid buffet, new since my last visit some years ago. A few minutes with J. Lelliott, Stationmaster, led to a pass being issued and I approached Southern 'Q' class 0-6-0 No 541, also in authentic black livery. Again a three-person crew made room for me: Driver John White, Fireman David Foale and Trainee A. Pinkess.

The 'Bluebell' route consists of an easy start from Sheffield Park, past the halt which was relocated from the top of Freshfield bank. Once into this climb, the gradient is a constant 1 in 75, then a short easy stretch, then a further 1 in 75 to Horsted Keynes station.

The 'Q' class were never regarded as particularly strong, but on this day No 541 made the run to time with a minimum of fuss. It was interesting to note that (as on *Swanage*) a steam reverser was provided; the 'Q' class is one of several with injector steam valves operated by pulling a lever, rather than turning a handwheel. (The injectors are situated below the footplate, the usual location on UK locomotives. However, all NZR live-steam injectors are of the lifting type, fitted by the side of the firebox and several feet above the cab floor.)

Driver White clearly did not intend to thrash his engine; Fireman Foale gave a well-considered display of economical firing, preferring to work with a hot, thin fire. After arriving at Horsted Keynes, I observed a superbly restored LBSCR 'Terrier' 0-6-0T with — mounted upon the smokebox door — a grotesque representation of a face, upon which I prefer not to comment.

Before leaving Horsted Keynes, I visited the carriage depot, guided by long-serving 'Bluebell' executive Roger Price. (Locomotive enthusiasts such as myself tend to forget that no carriages means no trains, which means no rail service.) The standard of workmanship was very high, particularly on the Pullman car then being overhauled. In addition to all the restoration work which I observed, the predominant topic — frequently raised — was the extension to East Grinstead. There was clear pride in what had been achieved (the first part of the new line is already open), and genuine excitement over what lies ahead. Completion of the project will bring the track's length up from under 5 miles to over 11, and will provide the vital link with BR. Much remains to be done, but Sharpthorne Tunnel and Imberhorne Viaduct are in remarkably good condition; excellent work has been carried out at Kingscote station.

My departure from the 'Bluebell' ended a week of superb hospitality which it was my very good fortune to enjoy. I count myself as lucky indeed to spend three days on five of Britain's best steam railways. To their managements and staff — who found the time to make me welcome while operating their lines so professionally — I am deeply indebted. Sincere thanks are due also to Glenda Arthur and Alan Russell for assistance with this article.

Finally, the Glenbrook Vintage Railway, and all the other NZ preserved lines, have made me most welcome. They would surely do the same for any other railway enthusiast who visited New Zealand.

16
North & West Signalling Today

Rhodri Clark

The railway between Newport and Shrewsbury, known as the North & West route, is one of only a few British main lines still largely controlled by semaphore signals. The signalling is made doubly interesting for the enthusiast by the legacies of the one-time joint ownership of the route north of Hereford.

After much legal wrangling, the Shrewsbury & Hereford Railway was operated by the LNWR and GWR from July 1862 (less than 10 years after its opening throughout), and later by the LMS and GWR. Even today, both the LMR and WR are involved with the line, since it crosses the regional boundary north of Craven Arms.

From 1872, interlocking signalling was installed on the joint line, most work being contracted to Saxby & Farmer, which supplied signalboxes to two designs that were exclusive to the LNWR/GWR joint lines. They are now labelled LNWR/GWR Joint Types 1 and 2 respectively. Both were related to contemporary S&F standard designs. Of the 15 boxes to the first design on the North & West, six now survive. There were three LNWR/GWR Joint Type 2 boxes in Hereford; only one remains.

Later signalling work saw the appearance of boxes to standard LNWR and GWR designs on the Shrewsbury and Hereford line, the former including a signalbox on a steel gantry above the tracks at Leominster station. Apart from the celebrated and massive Severn Bridge Junction signalbox at Shrewsbury, all the LNWR standard boxes on the

Above right:
The Abergavenny up home is pulled off for the passage of Evening Star with a special train on 24 April 1982. The short signal arm controls entry to the up goods loop. This bracket signal is something of a veteran, having been installed by Westinghouse during World War 2. Notice the unusual guy-wire, stretched between the signal and a post on the far side of the railway line.
A. P. Clark

Right:
The North & West line at Pontrilas, showing the McKenzie & Holland Type 3 signalbox, which was switched out on this Sunday afternoon. A class 116 DMU hurries past with the 16.35 Hereford to Cardiff Central local working.

All photographs taken by the author unless credited otherwise.

Left:
Hereford box, situated at the south end of the station. This is the only remaining example of the LNWR/GWR Joint Type 2 design, three of which were installed in Hereford in a resignalling project of 1884. A century later, a panel was installed in Ayleston Hill box (which had been renamed 'Hereford' in 1973), making Hereford the only concentration of colour-light signals on the North & West, excluding the area covered by Newport Panel and Little Mill Junction boxes.

Below left:
Moreton-on-Lugg signalbox is a late GWR replacement, of 1943. This design is known as Type 12A. Note the unusual roof.

Right:
The signalbox at Bromfield, built in 1873, is a good example of the LNWR/GWR Joint Type 1 design, with a base which is almost square at 16ft 6in x 15ft 6in. Leominster (South End) is of similar dimensions, while Woofferton Junction box is a larger variant of this design, measuring 36ft 10in x 16ft 8in.

Below:
Dating from 1931, the GWR Type 34 box at Craven Arms Crossing was previously one of three signalboxes at Craven Arms, at which time it was named 'Long Lane Crossing'. This box was selected for retention because it controls an adjacent level crossing. Consequently, the distant junction for the Central Wales line, at the far end of the station, had to be worked by Central Wales train guards until a point motor was installed recently.

North & West have disappeared, while a few GWR standard examples remain, including a handsome GWR Type 7 brick box, with hipped roof, at Sutton Bridge Junction, Shrewsbury.

The line south of Hereford, originally the Newport, Abergavenny & Hereford Railway route, was absorbed by the GWR in 1863. Nevertheless, a variety of signalboxes is also to be found here: GWR-designed at Abergavenny and, on the base of the previous box, at Tram Inn, and McKenzie & Holland Type 3 boxes at Pontrilas and Little Mill Junction. The last-named controls the remaining stub of the Pontypool to Monmouth line, open for freight as far as Glascoed, as well as interfacing with Newport Panel Box.

Many of the North & West signalboxes overlook level crossings, having been retained as block-posts in preference over others. The LNWR/GWR Joint Type 1 box guarding the level crossing at Onibury was replaced in 1977 by a small austere shed — literally a signalbox!

Over 70 boxes once controlled the line between Newport and Shrewsbury. Excluding Newport Panel Box, this total has been whittled down to 16. Although certain boxes are sometimes switched out, all those controlling crossings have to be manned whenever trains are running, and it seems likely that this labour-intensive manual signalling will, fairly soon, be swept away in the continual search for economy by Regional and Railfreight Sectors.

My thanks to Ray Caston for his assistance in the preparation of this article. Further details of the signalboxes described may be found in *The Signal Box* (OPC, 1986).

Above:

The signalbox and railway line north of Church Stretton station, with the old station building on the left. The 17.00 Manchester to Cardiff Sprinter (Class 155) passes an upper-quadrant home signal and the remains of a water crane. There is a mixture of upper and lower quadrant signals in this vicinity.

Left:

The smartly-kept LNWR/GWR Joint Type 1 signalbox at Marsh Brook. It contains an 18-lever locking frame.

Right:

The North & West line at Dorrington, with the LNWR/GWR Joint Type 1 signalbox in evidence. All the main line signals are cleared in this Sunday morning view, looking north.

Far right:

An interesting BR banner repeater south of Dorrington box on the up (northbound) line. It is required because the road bridge in the background restricts the driver's view of the nearest signal in the previous photograph.

17
Steam on the North Wales Coast

The decision by BR to add Crewe-Holyhead to the list of approved routes for steam operation and then give it a frequent summer service in 1989, has been one of the most exciting developments in main line steam in recent years. In the autumn of 1990 BR gilded this lily by passing several locomotives to work this route at 75mph, rather than the usual 60mph limit.

This feature is a pictorial celebration of steam workings on this photogenic main line.

Right:
On 16 September 1990, working the last 'North Wales Coast Express' of the season, Stanier Pacific No 6201 *Princess Elizabeth* **storms away from Chester and towards Roodee Junction.**
Doug Birmingham

Below:
'West Country' No 34027 *Taw Valley* **stands with the 'NWCE' under the train shed roof of Llandudno station on 16 July 1989, waiting to be drawn back to Llandudno Junction by diesel power before proceeding to Holyhead. In the following winter this fine example of an LNWR overall roof, dating from the 1890s, was almost completely demolished.** *Doug Birmingham*

Left:

The smallest engine so far to feature on the 'NWCE', 'Black five' No 5407 has proved itself master of this work as well as many other steam routes. It is seen heading smartly away from Llandudno on 28 August 1990. *Mike Matthews*

Left:

On 2 September 1990 *Princess Elizabeth* **tackles the climb past Llandulas on the outward journey of the 'NWCE'.** *Phil Chilton*

Below:

Princess Elizabeth **emerged through Conwy town walls with the return 'NWCE' on 2 September 1990.** *Phil Chilton*

Above left:

Homeward bound on 5 August 1990, BR Class 8 Pacific No 71000 Duke of Gloucester accelerates away from Rhyl, passing sad evidence of reduced facilities on this line, the lifted siding tracks and a much reduced signal gantry. The cast metal InterCity swallow emblem on the front lamp bracket is No 71000's personal embellishment.
Doug Blrmingham

Left:

Earlier that same day, No 71000 and its 14-coach train pulls away from Penmaenmawr station for Holyhead. *Doug Birmingham*

Above:

On 25 July 1990 No 71000 heads the return workng up the grade out of Holyhead station, passing the remains of the MPD on the *right.*
Doug Birmingham

Right:

On 13 October 1990, No 6201 *Princess Elizabeth* heads the Holyhead-bound 'Ynys Mon Express' into Bangor station's through road. This SLOA-sponsored train originated at Euston, unlike the BR-organised 'NWCEs', which start their journeys at Crewe. *Doug Birmingham*

Above:
The scenery and surroundings of the North Wales line make much of its attraction. The crossing of the River Conwy through Stephenson's fine tubular bridge and the sweep past Conwy Castle is one of the classic stretches. *Princess Elizabeth* brings the 'NWCE' out of the bridge and below the Castle walls on 2 September 1990. *Doug Birmingham*

Right:
The leaden light of a cloudy August late afternoon in 1989 gives a curious effect to this scene, with No 5407 bringing the return NWCE across the causeway between Conwy and Llandudno Junction. *J.H.Cooper-Smith*

Below right:
The 13 October 1990 'Ynys Mon Express' was delayed at Holyhead and was running 70min late at 18.25 as it tore through Colwyn Bay station, with *Princess Elizabeth* working hard to reach the 75mph speed limit, at which this was one of the first trains permitted to run. *Larry Goddard*

Facing page, top:
Anything can happen with BR steam today! 'A4' No 60009 leaves Colwyn Bay with a returning 'NWCE' on 21 August 1990, passing a 'heritage' DMU on a Bangor working. *Larry Goddard*

Facing page, bottom:
No 5407 storms away from Colwyn Bay with the returning 'NWCE' in the evening light of 9 September 1990. *Larry Goddard*

Photograph: Brian Dobbs